RESTORING
THE
WONDER

MIKE STARKEY is vicar of a multicultural church in north London and author of *God, Sex and Generation X* and *Fashion and Style*. A former radio journalist, he is widely known as one of Britain's most incisive Christian communicators. He was a finalist in *The Times* Preacher of the Year Award and contributes to the *Christian Herald* and London's Premier Radio. He is married to Naomi and they have two children, Joel and Joy.

RESTORING
THE
WONDER

MIKE STARKEY

TRIANGLE

First published in Great Britain in 1999
Triangle
Society for Promoting Christian Knowledge
Holy Trinity Church
Marylebone Road
London NW1 4DU

Scripture extracts are take from the
New International Version of the Bible,
copyright © 1973, 1978, 1984 by the
International Bible Society.
Published by Hodder & Stoughton.
On page 79, lines from W. H. Auden's
For the Time Being are reprinted by
permission of the publishers, Faber & Faber.

British Library Cataloguing-in-Publication Data

A catalogue record for this book is available from
the British Library

ISBN 0-281-05210-7

Typeset by Pioneer Associates, Perthshire
Printed in Great Britain by
Caledonian International Ltd, Glasgow

CONTENTS

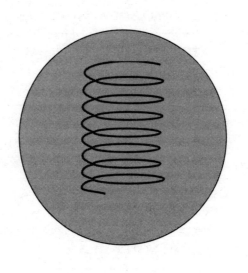

CHAPTER ONE

THE SPIRAL OF UNWONDER

A man who has lost his sense of wonder is a man dead.

(William of St Thierry, 1085–1148)

Too bored to live

It is February. The sky is overcast with the bland grey of an English winter. There is a chill in the air. The scene is Woodford Green, a village located at the point where the suburban sprawl of north-east London meets the open countryside of Essex.

Gordon Colbourne, local firefighter, is sitting by the window of his fire station, watching the world go by. His gaze follows a man walking down the street. The man stops near the fire station. Through the window Colbourne notices the man is holding a shotgun. He watches in growing horror as the man turns the shotgun on himself and pulls the trigger. A shot rings out and a body slumps to the ground. Colbourne runs to his aid. When he reaches the man, he finds that despite his wounds, he is still conscious. He is clearly in pain. But the injured man's dominant emotion appears to be anger: 'Why didn't it work?' he stammers. 'I want to die.'

Another firefighter, Stuart Jones, rushes out with a resuscitator, hoping to help keep the man alive until an

1

ambulance arrives. Three times, the man pushes the life-saving equipment away, begging the fireman instead to pick up the gun and finish him off. They try other forms of first aid, but with each attempt the man insists they do not touch him. He pleads, 'I want to die. Leave me alone.'

The name of the wounded man is Colin Bensley. He is a 46-year-old self-made millionaire with a fine home in Kew, a picturesque area of south London. He had made his fortune as a computer consultant and retired from work ten years earlier. He appears to have it all. He has achieved what most of us long for: a partner, a fine home, success and the wealth to live a life of leisure.

Appearances, however, can deceive. The reality is that the interior of Bensley's gilded life has been hollow for many years. Since his retirement he has been bored. Life no longer has challenge, colour, purpose. The wonder has gone. He travels to Woodford Green, where his wife works as an accountant. He phones her to say he will not be home when she returns. He makes his way to the street outside her office where, in a final dramatic gesture, he shoots himself. When his suicide bid appears to have failed, he begs his would-be rescuers to finish him off. He is too bored to live any longer. He later dies of his injuries. A tragic end to ten years lived on the spiral of unwonder.[1]

The world's sweetheart

The scene is Hollywood. It is the golden age of the silent film. The screen idol of the day is Canadian-born Mary Pickford. By 1916, at the age of 23, Pickford has become the highest-paid star in the history of the silent screen. During the 1920s and early 1930s she is known as 'the world's sweetheart' and her fame is only equalled by the president and baseball superstar Babe Ruth. In

1920 she becomes co-founder of United Artists, along with Charlie Chaplin and Douglas Fairbanks.

But fame can be fickle. By 1927 a movie revolution is underway, with the first-ever talking picture: *The Jazz Singer*. Despite predictions by Charlie Chaplin that the new fad will not last, and grumbles from an industry forced to invest in new sound studios, it is not long before silent films are replaced by the 'talkies'. Pickford's own popularity wanes alongside the medium which brought her success.

For a woman whose life and emotions had been inextricably bound to her public profile, the loss of celebrity proves devastating. She begins to drink heavily. It is soon clear to everyone that Mary Pickford is an alcoholic. From the 1930s to her death in 1979, at the age of 86, Mary Pickford lives on, self-pitying, almost constantly drunk. One friend comments that during all those years she never once sees her sober. Forty-four years with nothing to live for, hopeless, joyless. Forty-four years on the spiral of unwonder.

A withered leaf

The great scientist sits in his book-lined study. The tables are piled with notebooks, sketches and letters. On the cluttered shelves sit rows of mysterious bottles, jars and boxes, while the window offers a panorama over the apple orchard. Charles Darwin has become the towering figure of contemporary science. He first gained acclaim among the scientific community in the 1830s, following his five-year voyage of discovery around the world on HMS *Beagle*. Wider celebrity followed the publication of his first major work, *On the Origin of Species*, in 1859 and his controversial bestseller, *The Descent of Man*, in 1871.

It is now the late 1870s. Darwin spends his closing years at the home where he and his wife have spent their married life and raised their family – Down House, set amid the woods and valleys of rural Kent. It is a fine English country residence with green shutters, a summerhouse and a stream running close by. Letters pour in daily from admiring correspondents around the world, asking his opinion on all matters from naturalism to religion. He sits in the room the family calls 'the New Study', his mind immersed in the science which has been his lifetime obsession.

But Darwin is unable to savour the rural landscape or relax with the trappings of fame. He confides to close friends and to his diary that the joy has gone. Once, he writes, he could enjoy the beauty of the natural world, poetry and literature. Now these simple pleasures leave him unmoved. There was a time when he loved music but now, he says, 'my soul is too dried up to appreciate it as in old days ... I am a withered leaf for every subject except science. It sometimes makes me hate science.'[2]

It is as if the very scientific enterprise which had been his life's mission has turned from adrenaline to anaesthetic in his veins. The world is still full of music, art and beauty, but somehow Darwin has become numbed to it all. He is no longer able to sense the wonder of life. The joy has gone. He spends his closing years at Down House regretful, desensitized to all but the day's work. Charles Darwin: a great intellect; but a life ebbing away on the spiral of unwonder.

The malady of the age

Charles Darwin, Mary Pickford, Colin Bensley. Three people who appeared to have gained the world, but apparently at the cost of losing something more valuable in the process. Three people who, somewhere along the line, lost the wonder of life: the shiver down the spine, the twinkle in the eye, the spring in the step.

4

Three people who had scaled the summit which most of us are aiming at, only to find the view was not worth seeing.

Many people today will see their own lives mirrored here. The young mum who feels her life slipping away in a blur of soiled nappies and damp cloths. The promising student who sits in the college bar drinking the days away, unable to envisage any better future worth studying for. The newly retired teacher in a state of shocked bereavement at losing routine, identity and purpose. The church leader who preaches the joy of the Lord, but at home sits gazing into a dark chasm separating public rhetoric from personal reality. The elderly woman who lives alone in the grim tower-block, afraid to go outside, cherishing her memories of a more civilized age and friends long dead. The young man in a dead-end restaurant job, who feels life is passing him by. Surely there must be more to life than this. But what? All are victims of the great malady of our age: the loss of wonder.

LIFE IN ALL ITS DULLNESS

Human life begins in passion, is nurtured in hope and delivered in awe. First-time parents frequently find themselves staring open-mouthed at their new child, scarcely able to believe such an event could have happened. Something so alive, so much a part of them, yet so separate from them too. A gift. A miracle. A source of wonder. No fanfare is too grand to herald the eminent arrival. The child is held with the careful delicacy of fine china, lest its fragile and wonderful life slip from their grasp. Sleepless nights are spent watching over the infant: sometimes to marvel, sometimes from anxious concern. As it grows the child is fed, educated, clothed, entertained. This new life must be given the best possible start. This restless bundle of unrealized potential must be shaped.

At last, the child is ready to embark on adult life, the culmination of all those years of preparation. Here, finally, is the big one: the great drama of adulthood, for which everything else has been a rehearsal. And on the stage of life, the young adult finds . . . what?

Here, the true nature of the drama starts to become all too evident. A bland and unfulfilling job, a series of unsatisfying relationships, long evenings in front of the TV, a circuit of mindless routines lacking either direction or purpose. Life is neither a melodrama nor a comedy. It is a tragedy. With Shakespeare's tragic hero Macbeth, many arrive at the resigned conclusion:

> Life's but a walking shadow, a poor player,
> That struts and frets his hour upon the stage,
> And then is heard no more; it is a tale
> Told by an idiot, full of sound and fury,
> Signifying nothing.[3]

The plot of a bad novel

One of today's foremost humorists is Garrison Keillor, best known for his wry tales from the fictional Minnesota town of Lake Wobegon. One of Keillor's comic creations is the failed Western novelist called Dusty Pages, who sits mulling over why his writing career never took off. He recalls the plot of one of his Westerns, *Giddup Beauty! C'mon Big Girl, Awaaaaaayy!*:

> Buck rides two thousand miles across blazing deserts searching for Julie Ann and finally, after killing twenty men and wearing out three mounts and surviving two avalanches, a prairie fire, a blizzard, and a passel of varmints, he finds her held captive by the bloodthirsty Arapaho. 'So, how are you doing?' he asks her. 'Oh, all right, I guess,' she says, gazing up

at him, wiping the sweat from her brow. 'You want to come in for a cup of coffee?' 'Naw, I just wanted to make sure you were okay. You *look* okay.' 'Yeah, I lost some weight, about twenty pounds.' 'Oh, really. How?' 'Eating toads and grasshoppers.' 'Uh-huh. Well, now that I look at you, you do look lighter.' 'Sure you won't have coffee?' 'Naw, I gotta ride. Be seein' ya, now.' 'Okay, bye!'[4]

To many, the plot of Keillor's bad Western is unnervingly like that of life. You are squeezed, struggling, into the world. You overcome incredible obstacles. You negotiate illnesses, accidents, the perils of the world for a growing child. You spend years preparing, preparing.

And finally you get there. Adult life. You have arrived.

But soon you look around in puzzlement. Is this *it*? Shouldn't there be, well, more than this? Is this really what everything's been leading up to? It feels suspiciously like the plot of an ineptly written novel. A tale told by somebody with a fair knack for building up suspense, only to lose his way during the course of the book.

Author Isaac Bashevis Singer wrote that 'life is God's great novel'. The fact that so many lives are bored and aimless, including the lives of many who claim religious faith, hardly seems to reflect well on the plot-writing skills of the novelist. In the words of Woody Allen, 'If it turns out that there is a God, I don't think that he's evil. But the worst you can say about him is that basically he's an underachiever.'[5]

A SEARCH FOR LOST WONDER

Yet something deep within most of us rebels against the bleak conclusion that life is nothing more than a boring plot by a bad novelist. We crave a sense that there is more to life. We yearn for a joy we feel ought to be there, to taste a wonder promised but not delivered. We want excitement, passion and purpose.

Wonder off the shelf

This is the backdrop to today's multi-billion dollar advertising industry.[6] Since the early post-war years, the main tool of advertisers has been the marketing of dreams. Few ads today attempt to persuade us of the practical benefits or the technical superiority of a product. Instead, we are offered imaginative dream-scapes in which our cravings may run wild. Brands are given 'personalities', in which consumers see reflected an image of themselves as they would most like to be: beautiful, content, popular, purposeful, in love.

Psychographics rose to prominence in the early 1970s as the science of matching dreams to consumer groups. Not everybody shares the same vision of the good life. Not everybody finds a sense of wonder in the same places or experiences. So the advertising industry has increasingly called on the insights of psychologists in targeting its dreams. Psychographics is about finding the right buttons to press. For one group, visions of wonder may be evoked by a rural idyll, with rolling meadows and roses around the cottage door; for others it is a stark cityscape and cool trainers.

Whatever the specifics of each campaign, one factor remains constant: the message that the wonder-filled life is just one purchase away. Product, publicist and purchaser are co-conspirators, fellow travellers in a search for lost wonder. We are bidding to buy; they, eager to sell.

You might expect that as a consequence we would be the happiest, most wonder-filled society in history.

Never have the desires of so many been so thoroughly identified, minutely analysed and assiduously satisfied. Today's suburbanite enjoys a level of personal comfort beyond that of royalty in earlier centuries. Mass production and a restless fashion industry have made available to us more colours, textures and styles than in any civilization in history. We have more opportunities for entertainment than ever, access to more learning, more religions, more foods. We know about a wider range of sexual options, we have access to a finer network of transport and communications.

Yet our agonizing paradox is that our culture appears to have less of a sense of the wonder of life than any other in history. A cursory glance at the lives of the rich and famous even appears to show an infuriating inverse equation: more things, less wonder. A sure route to losing all wonder is to become a movie star or a Lottery winner – if media profiles of such people are to be believed.

There seems to be no discernible link between the level of our comfort and affluence and the level of our wonder. Some are poor and wonderless, some poor and wonder-filled. Some are rich and wonderless, a few rich and wonder-filled. It appears our consumer culture has been deceiving us. But such is its potency, and our willingness to participate in the bluff, that we raise no outcry. We simply move on to desiring the next product, hoping against hope that this one will finally bring the wonder we are searching for.

There only appears to be one discernible constant in this wild-goose chase: more possessions will bring no measurable increase in personal joy, satisfaction or wonder, unless we have first learned to value what we already have. Our grandmothers told us to count our blessings. But in a consumer society which follows a creed of permanent dissatisfaction, counting blessings is heresy. Your grandmother, after all, is not the one making the ads.

Trying other keys

The pursuit of affluence, then, seems not to be a guaranteed path to restored wonder. But maybe there is some other crucial factor that will help us in our search. Perhaps the key lies in intelligence, temperament or religion?

Intelligence

It would be natural to expect those with a high IQ and a lively mind to have a more wonder-filled response to life. They, after all, are the ones who thrive most on mental stimulation.

But evidence for this is in short supply. If anything, people's experience shows that the equation seems inverse, like that between affluence and wonder. Intellectuals, from my own experience, are as prone to a mind-set of boredom and indifference as any other group – often more so. Many great philosophers have been great melancholics. For countless leading thinkers, a keen mind simply means an ability to see the unwonder of their own lives with greater clarity.

Some are intellectual and wonderless, some intellectual and wonder-filled. Some are slow-witted and wonderless, some slow-witted and wonder-filled. Again, a single constant seems to emerge: to have a higher IQ will bring no measurable increase in personal joy, satisfaction or wonder unless we have first learned to look with wonder at the life, world and people which are the object of our study.

Temperament

So the answer does not seem to lie in intelligence. But

10

perhaps having a particular personality or temperament will steer us towards wonder. Could it be that some people are more prone to finding wonder in life? Quiet, contemplative types, perhaps? Or noisy extroverts?

Again, evidence indicates otherwise. Some contemplatives have a heightened sensitivity to the wonder of life. Others use a reflective temperament to reflect on how miserable they feel. At the same time, some with an extrovert personality might be noisy and outgoing because their hearts are overflowing with wonder, whereas others may use their natural exuberance to mask a profound inner emptiness.

The only constant appears to be this: whether you are one of nature's extroverts or introverts, whether you are exuberant or reclusive, none of these alone will bring any measurable increase in personal joy, satisfaction or wonder unless you have first found a key to the gate of wonder. Our personal volume control does not double as a wonder-regulator.

Religion

If wonder is not a by-product of either affluence, intelligence or temperament, the answer must surely lie in religion. After all, religions by definition concern themselves with ultimate questions of purpose, fulfilment and inner peace. The search for lost wonder ought to end here, with a simple assertion that the more religious you are, the more wonder-filled your life must be.

Not necessarily. As we shall discover, the question of God is inseparable from the quest for wonder. And we shall find themes and characters from the Bible offering unique insights into where wonder might be found. So, in one sense, the loss of wonder is a profoundly religious question, and only ultimate answers will be big enough to satisfy. On the other hand, religion clearly does not automatically produce wonder. Indeed, it frequently does quite the opposite. Some of the most miserable and wonderless people are religious. Some of the most judgemental, unkind and unfriendly in our communities are regular in worship and punctilious in doctrine.

Once again, a depressingly familiar constant seems to emerge: filling our days with religious activities and dogma does not necessarily increase personal joy, satisfaction or wonder. Again, the only option seems to be succumbing to the malady of the age: numbing down.

A hopeless quest?

The search for a key which unlocks our sense of wonder appears to be a hopeless one. None of the keys offered by our society appears to fit. We can be affluent, intelligent, highly religious, with a personality which is either wildly vivacious or quietly contemplative, and still live on a spiral of unwonder. Little surprise, then, that many view their own lack of wonder as a normal condition of existence. We have grown used to seeing the wallpaper of life as grey and patternless. We have given up asking whether our own eyesight might be faulty. None of the remedial treatments which promise a fresh clarity of vision seems to work.

The issue for many, then, becomes this: granted that existence is basically drab, how are we going to kick-start ourselves back to life again? Some are prepared to take increasingly drastic measures to halt the slide into blandness.

AM I STILL ALIVE?

The actor Matt Le Blanc has become a hero for a generation. By the time of writing this book, the TV sitcom *Friends*, in which he plays the babe-crazed, dim-witted Joey, had topped the UK ratings and was at number three in the USA. The thirty-something star is typical of his generation in his love of extreme or dangerous pastimes, particularly snowboarding, fast cars and motorbikes. He confessed to a British newspaper, 'I'm an adrenaline junkie. Love speed. I sky-dive as well. It's like banging your head against a brick wall just because it feels so good when you stop. Afterwards, it's so life-affirming. "Oh man," you think. "I'm still alive. Wow!"'[7]

Other popular high-risk hobbies include bungee jumping, rock climbing, pot-holing, travelling in war-zones, jet-biking and white-water rafting. Fairground rides have changed from sedate carousels to white-knuckle heart-stoppers. Our TV screens are full of re-enactments of vicious, real-life crimes and hospital dramas. In a number of universities and colleges, the Dangerous Sports Club is among the most fashionable on campus. Extreme sports are moving increasingly from the fringes to the mainstream. Some 10,000 people attended the UK's first dangerous sports weekend for all the family at Donington Park. The event was billed as 'a chance to experience the ultimate adrenaline buzz on land, sea and in the air'.

High-risk hobbies offer two things. One is a promise of jump-starting a life that has stalled. The sensation of intense physical pain, exhilaration or a sudden, violent rush of adrenaline reassure us that we can still *feel*. They offer reassurance to numbed or desensitized people that they are still alive, that all is not lost, that life can still hold thrills.

The other point of dangerous pastimes is their promise of a day-trip to the shores of death, but with a fair certainty that we will return home without taking the plunge. We return scared, gasping, with a renewed gratitude for life, even our meagre, dull life on the spiral of unwonder. It is this sense of gratitude that forms such a crucial component of our capacity for wonder – as we shall explore later.

There is disturbing evidence that some people are also using violent and life-threatening sexual practices to stimulate arousal. In recent years, a number of high-profile cases have hit the headlines. Doctors say severe oxygen deprivation can in some cases heighten erotic sensation, and many people seem willing to accept the risk of death through asphyxia for the promise of a more intense thrill.

Pity the man or woman who stuffs their heart with money, possessions, learning, religions and sex, but still finds it empty. Pity a generation of people living on the spiral of unwonder, who find that even the most extreme pleasures and pains do little to alleviate the numbness.

Complacent about life

Perhaps one of the main reasons why people are drawn to flirting with danger and near-death experiences is that ours is a generation with the unprecedented luxury of being complacent about life. For most of us, death (real death, not sanitized movie death) is largely alien territory. A stroll through any old churchyard, reading inscriptions on gravestones, gives a fascinating glimpse into bygone days. Most families lost several infants in childbirth or early childhood. Those who survived frequently succumbed to a range of illnesses, and even those living to a ripe old age had far shorter life-spans than we expect today. Average life expectancy in seventeenth-century England was 23 years. Only five per cent of the population made it beyond the age of 60. By the eighteenth century, life expectancy was 43 years for the upper classes, 30 for tradesmen and just 22 for labourers.[8]

Massive improvements in medicine and sanitation

have made childbirth safer, eliminated the risk of many major illnesses and prolonged life. On average, we reach our 40s before we experience the death of a close family member, and would feel cheated if we died before today's average age of death: our late 70s. For over half a century there have been no prolonged wars likely to involve people we know. Most of us encounter few reminders of the fragility of life. We are rarely prompted to reflect that life itself is a precious gift, which might be snatched away at any moment. Sudden, unexpected death – from a child at the seaside to an English princess – arrives like a bolt of lightning from a clear sky.

My wife and I recently read her grandmother's diaries, from the early years of the twentieth century. What struck us most was the ever-present shadow of death: through infant mortality, sickness and war. It is hard to imagine my wife's grandmother seeing the point of bungee jumping or sky-diving to appreciate life afresh. Her generation, like most before, could do no other than experience life as a rare and precious commodity. Perhaps this helps explain the odd fact that many who lived through the Second World War look back on it as the happiest period of their lives. Something about the ever-present shadow of death appears to have made every day a moment of wonder, to be lived to the full and shared selflessly with others.

Are we to conclude, then, that the only sure way to restore wonder is to engineer artificial flirtations with death, or move to a war-zone? Can we not find a way to restore lost wonder without daily endangering our lives? That is the central quest of this book. As we begin that quest in earnest, our first clue will be to look more closely at the spiral of unwonder.

THE SPIRAL OF UNWONDER

To lose a sense of life's wonder is like living on a downward spiral. A spiral makes two types of movement simultaneously. One is a circular motion: life on the spiral of unwonder turns round and round, just as our lives have their own particular cycles and seasons. But a spiral is not a circle: it moves not only round, but also onwards, just like our lives.

In practice, there are three major components on each circuit of the spiral of unwonder, each in turn feeding and aggravating the other. These three are: indifference, fantasy and withdrawal. The spiral can be illustrated as follows:

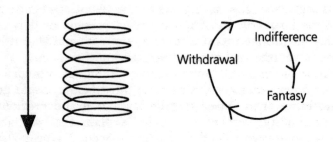

Indifference

The spiral of unwonder starts in a growing mood of indifference to life. What I have fails to excite me as it once did, and my response to life becomes increasingly apathetic. The word 'apathy' comes from a Greek and Latin root meaning 'without feelings', and it is this loss of feeling which characterizes life on the spiral. Like Darwin in his closing years at Down House, the people who have lost a sense of wonder find their response to the stimuli of life has become dulled. Their *joie-de-vivre* has gone.

At its most serious, this loss of feeling can become

acute paralysis, desensitizing us to the whole spectrum of life experiences: such as our present circumstances, the place we live, our capacity to appreciate and enjoy the present moment, our wonder towards God, our possessions, our work, and the way we feel about the people around us. In this book, we shall focus on the first three of these: place, time and God. We shall aim to establish principles for escaping from the spiral of unwonder which might then be applied to other areas of life – such as possessions, work and people.

Our numbing usually happens unnoticed, over a long period of time. In this sense, indifference works differently from wonder. We rarely drift unawares into joy, commitment or wonder. Positives tend to jump out at us when we least expect them, bringing a sudden leap to the heart and smile to the lips. People are often – in the memorable phrase C. S. Lewis borrowed from Wordsworth – surprised by joy.

But we can drift into indifference. People who find they have become indifferent to joy can rarely put a date on the moment when wonder was stolen. Indifference is not a conversion experience. Instead, we look back and see how our zest for life, our passion for our partner and the joy of living in our neighbourhood all appear to have ebbed away, slowly and imperceptibly.

The word 'indifferent' also has a Latin root. It means 'making no distinction'. The person who lives on the spiral of unwonder no longer distinguishes the exciting from the bland, the meaningful from the meaningless. Over a period of time, the primary colours of life become hidden behind an impenetrable grey mist. All distinctions become hazy, our senses numbed.

Fantasy

Yet few of us are content to live a life of grey indifference. We persist in believing there ought to be more to life. So the same movement which begins in indifference soon spirals round into fantasy. What we have has not brought the wonder we crave. It stands to reason, then, that wonder must lie in what we do not have. Fantasy is feeding our pet 'If Onlys'.

Each of us has a pet 'If Only' living in our imagination. In its early years the 'If Only' is a small, lovable creature who looks at its owner wide-eyed, begging to be fed. To begin with, the cute 'If Only' makes an endearing pet, bounding around the fertile fields of our imagination, full of energy and affection. But as it grows, the 'If Only' begins to lose its cuteness. Little by little it can grow into a monster with an insatiable appetite. No matter how much we feed it, it still demands more.

A pet 'If Only' can have different names at different times. Here are a few: Lottery win, Adultery, Escape, Career advancement, Supercool image, New kitchen. We feed them as we fill our imaginations with fantasies which tell us that we should be happier *if only* we were somewhere else than we are, *if only* we had more cash than we currently have, *if only* we were with somebody other than the person we are with, *if only* we looked different, *if only* now was a time other than the present moment.

In time, the monster can grow so large that it fills the imagination which is its home. And still it demands to be fed. By this stage, it is no longer clear who is the owner, who the pet. The 'If Only' has taken over the entire imagination. When this happens, the whole person is left with no desire at all to be herself. She sees nothing in her own life or circumstances worth keeping. She fills her mind with fantasies of escape. This may take the form of an obsession with a favourite movie star, or a TV or sports personality. It may be the oblivion offered by drugs or alcohol.

Anything to fill the gnawed, hollowed-out centre of her life once the wonder has gone.

Withdrawal

We grow indifferent to what we have. We fantasize about being anywhere else, with anybody else, at any time other than the present. The next turn of the spiral is that we withdraw even further from what we have. As a pet 'If Only' nibbles away at our wonder, the result is that we feel even less enthusiastic about our present circumstances. So we pull away emotionally. This in turn means we become still more indifferent to what we have. We descend the spiral of unwonder, down through indifference, fantasy and withdrawal and back to indifference again. Round and round, down and down we slide. A couple of simple illustrations will demonstrate the point.

Peter has lived in inner-city north London for several years, but he finds the area boring and uninspiring (indifference). So he dreams of what life might be like in rural Scotland, a cabin in the Rocky Mountains, or in a village on the Devon coast (fantasy). But the more he lingers in his fantasies of escape to a rural idyll, the less inspiring he finds his real surroundings in north London (withdrawal).

Sandra has been married to Mick for ten years. Familiarity has led to her taking him for granted, and she has begun to find the predictability of their relationship dull (indifference). She imagines what it would be like to have a whirlwind romance with a man with the sensitivity and passion Mick now lacks (fantasy). As she feeds her 'If Only', marriage to Mick looks all the more insipid by comparison. So her commitment to it declines (withdrawal).

Peter and Sandra are each living on their spirals of

unwonder: indifference feeding fantasy...feeding withdrawal...feeding indifference...feeding fantasy... feeding withdrawal. On and on, unless the spiral can be halted.

A LIFE ON THE SPIRAL: ECCLESIASTES

The late twentieth century has produced powerful portraits of life on the spiral of unwonder. Many of our novelists, film-makers, artists and philosophers have known what it feels like to live a life of unwonder, and they have left a profound and chilling legacy of protest against the unwonder of existence.

Still, perhaps the most devastating picture of unwonder we possess comes not from the contemporary arts, but an ancient book called Ecclesiastes. It is a strange, unsettling book. We do not know for certain who wrote it, nor even when it was written. But in its 12 short chapters, it succeeds in capturing all the blandness, futility and paralysis of a life from which the wonder has been drained:

> I have seen all the things that are done under the sun; all of them are meaningless, a chasing after the wind...I applied myself to the understanding of wisdom, and also of madness and folly, but I learned that this, too, is a chasing after the wind...The wise man has eyes in his head, while the fool walks in darkness; but I came to realise that the same fate overtakes them both. (Ecclesiastes 1.14, 17; 2.14).

So it goes on, an almost unremittingly dark meditation on the pointlessness of life, made all the more depressing since its author has clearly tried all three of the apparently promising routes off the spiral of unwonder. He is affluent. He is intelligent. He is religious. He has

20

tried all these things, but the only sound perspective on life, he finds, is a resigned nihilism.

The most extraordinary thing about Ecclesiastes, however, is how this ancient poem of unwonder has come down to us. It is in the Bible.

So who is this ancient cynic, who seems to have known for himself the agony of life lived on the spiral of unwonder? The work itself does not name him, referring to him by the Hebrew *qohelet*, or teacher. Our word 'Ecclesiastes' is simply a Greek translation of Qohelet. But the historical figure whose name has always been linked to the work is Solomon, king of Israel and philosopher of wisdom. A Jewish tradition claims Solomon wrote three books of the Bible. As a young man in love, he wrote the Song of Songs (also known as the Song of Solomon), in maturity and wisdom he wrote Proverbs (described in the opening verse as 'The proverbs of Solomon, son of David, king of Israel'). Finally, in the closing years of his life, a weary and jaded old man, he wrote Ecclesiastes.

There are clues in the book which make this plausible. Qohelet is introduced as a teacher or philosopher, son of King David, and king in Jerusalem (1.1). The voice is clearly that of an elderly man, approaching the end of life (12.1–7), wanting to share his personal reflections with a younger audience. And much of the content reflects experiences of Solomon: his unprecedented wealth (2.4–11), the size of his harem (2.8), his constant search for wisdom (1.12–18, 2.12–16).

Many scholars claim that the literary style of the book points to a date later than the tenth century BC, when Solomon was alive. Certainly, the book as it stands cannot be entirely from his pen. The voice of a second narrator (who speaks of Qohelet in the third person) introduces the meditation (1.1–11) and then concludes it (12.8–14). No doubt Ecclesiastes as we

21

have it now is a crafted literary piece, shaped and in part written by a later editor. But Jewish and Christian traditions agree that the wisdom-meditation he edited has roots in the time of King Solomon, and reflects the life-situation of Solomon in old age.

The historical account of Solomon's later years is not found in Ecclesiastes, but in 1 Kings 11. There we find the portrait of a once-great king who has lost the plot in old age, largely due to a combination of sex and esoteric religion.

It is a classic portrait of a man on the spiral of unwonder, a sad picture of infidelity which contrasts starkly with the eager commitments of his earlier years. By the time he was old, Solomon had no fewer than 700 wives of royal birth – mostly for the purpose of establishing treaties with other nations – and 300 concubines (1 Kings 11.1). This violated both the divine ban on kings taking more than one wife (Deuteronomy 17.17) and the biblical prohibition on marrying wives from Israel's ungodly neighbours (Exodus 34.15–16). It also entailed being unfaithful to his wife, the former princess of Egypt (1 Kings 3.1).

It is a classic portrait of a man grown bored with his wealth, his wife, his achievements, his gift of wisdom, even the God whose Temple he built – and with whom he has had awesome encounters on two separate occasions (1 Kings 3.4–5; 9.1–9). Unlike his passionate father David, Solomon becomes *indifferent*. When what he has fails to excite, he pursues all the forbidden pleasures his imagination can muster: he becomes sexually and religiously promiscuous in a vain bid to rekindle the wonder. He turns to *fantasy*. As a consequence, he drifts further and further from his earlier marital and spiritual commitments. Solomon *withdraws*.

Ecclesiastes offers an archetypal portrait of unwonder. A man who gains the world but loses himself in the process. A teacher of philosophy who carries on teaching wisdom long after his own capacity for joy, awe and wonder has evaporated and has been replaced by sex, political opportunism and consumer religion.

It is hardly surprising that the weary, jaded voice of Solomon sounds so familiar to a wonderless generation, living almost 3000 years later. We too can find nothing new under the sun. All our apparent momentum turns out to have been a chasing after the wind.

No escape from the spiral?

For many people today the road travelled by King Solomon, Charles Darwin, Mary Pickford and Colin Bensley seems to have a tragic inevitability about it. The spiral of unwonder descends. Joy ebbs away. Senses grow numbed. The descent takes place hour by hour in suburban semis, palaces, tower-blocks and cottages – in village, town and city alike. If the loss of wonder is the great malady of our age, our attempts to find a cure by accumulating more money and possessions, by developing our minds, by trying ever more bizarre and violent sexual practices, and by spending time in a blur of religious activities, fail to achieve what we hoped for. Even the adrenaline rush of dangerous sports fades in time – assuming we survive long enough for life to grow numb.

But from time to time, we may glimpse an alternative possibility. We meet a colleague who somehow seems to have retained a real sense of joy, a worshipper caught up in genuinely awestruck adoration, a neighbour full of fun and energy, a marriage which is committed and life-enhancing for both partners, a child for whom life is full of enchantment. How do these people fit into the picture? Perhaps they are hopelessly naive. Perhaps they have not yet joined the downward spiral, but will soon join the rest of us there.

There is another possibility. What if the spiral of unwonder is not the only spiral in life? What if there is also a spiral of wonder, a spiral which takes us ever upwards into higher reaches of joy and spontaneity? What if some people have learned the secret of living on a spiral of wonder? That is the awesome possibility we shall explore in the next chapter.

CHAPTER TWO

THE SPIRAL
OF WONDER

Is ditchwater dull? Naturalists with microscopes
have told me that it teems with quiet fun.

(G. K. Chesterton, *The Spice of Life*)

DEFINING WONDER

What is wonder? So far we have been gazing, perplexed,
into the gap left by its absence. We must now try to
define more closely what it means to have a sense of
wonder about life. First, a note of caution. We need to
approach this task with trepidation, trusting that our
zeal to understand wonder will not kill the very thing
we desire – like pinning down a rare butterfly, or
explaining a joke to the point where its humour dies.

For the English journalist and author G. K. Chesterton,
wonder is essentially a capacity for being surprised by
the brute fact of life itself. In his autobiography, he tells
how he was wrenched from the fashionable pessimism
of the late nineteenth century by a sense of gratitude
that life existed at all:

At the back of our brains, so to speak, there was a
forgotten blaze or burst of astonishment at our own
existence. The object of the artistic and spiritual life
was to dig for this submerged sunrise of wonder; so

25

that a man sitting in a chair might suddenly understand that he was actually alive, and be happy.[1]

For Chesterton, wonder arises from our learning to
look closely at the ordinary and discovering that it is in
fact quite extraordinary.

It is this sense of astonishment which also strikes
the nineteenth-century novelist and clergyman Charles
Kingsley. For him, a sense of wonder enables us to see
even the most basic aspects of existence as occasions
for awe: 'It is a strange thing, and a mystery, how we
ever got into this world, a stranger thing still to me
how we shall ever get out of this world again. Yet they
are common things enough – birth and death.'[2]

William Temple, one-time Archbishop of Canterbury,
extends to the created order this sense of amazement at
the fact of existence. Wonder, he writes, is a sense of
curiosity and awe about the world around us, which
forms the basis of all investigation of nature – whether
scientific or artistic: 'It is wonder that prompts the
mind to examine its environment'.[3] Nobel scientist
Albert Einstein agrees. For him, this sense of marvelling
and wondering is 'at the cradle of true art and science',[4]
and without it both disciplines – along with humanity
itself – will wither: 'Whoever is devoid of the capacity
to wonder, whoever remains unmoved, whoever cannot
contemplate or know the deep shudder of the soul in
enchantment, might just as well be dead for he has
already closed his eyes upon life.'[5]

Some writers go further, and see wonder as the
capacity to sense something mysterious or magical in
existence and the world around us. For the First World
War poet-priest, Geoffrey Studdert-Kennedy, wonder is
a person's realization that 'they live in the presence of
something greater, outside and beyond themselves'.[6]
The same impulse is echoed by the spiritual writer,

Carlo Carretto: 'For is not wonder the first, unconscious meeting with mystery? Does not wonder give birth to the first prayer? Does not the power to contemplate involve first the power to be awed?'[7]

The American Rollo May writes from the perspective of a secular psychologist, defining wonder as a person's realization that they have unlimited horizons and unbounded potential. But for May, too, a sense of wonder grows from the realization that there are mysteries in life as yet undiscovered. Wonder is 'essentially an "opening" attitude – an awareness that there is more to life than one has yet fathomed, an experience of new vistas in life to be explored as well as new profundities to be plumbed.'[8]

Each of these definitions rings true. In part, this is because we recognize in them the very things we lack. We have explored how life on the spiral of unwonder means feeling bored about existence, indifferent to the world and the people around us, a vague wishing that things were different from the way they are, and a consequent withdrawal into ourselves. This is the opposite end of a spectrum to the kind of wonder Chesterton, Einstein and the others discovered.

The challenge, then, is whether we can learn to cultivate one set of attitudes and not the other. To do this, we need to look closer at the spiral of wonder itself.

As we listen to the insights of those who have found wonder restored, and as we see the example of joyful, awestruck lives, we discover that a sense of wonder appears to have three component parts. It involves fresh encounter with the miracle of being alive and with the world around us, a fresh sense of gratitude for these things, and a fresh sense of commitment to living passionately, and to digging for life's buried treasures. Encounter, gratitude, commitment. These three, closely linked elements together form the spiral of wonder.

The upward spiral

Unlike the spiral of unwonder, the spiral which turns through encounter, gratitude and commitment spirals upwards. Rather than dragging us inexorably downwards, it lifts us ever higher. It can be illustrated as follows:

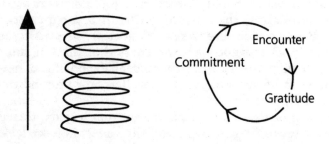

If the spiral of unwonder begins in a growing mood of indifference to the things around me, the spiral of wonder begins in a fresh and dynamic encounter with those same things.

The first mistake

The most common mistake made by people searching for lost wonder is to assume wonder is a by-product of circumstances. In other words, they assume that we are just passive receivers of a wonder which is sparked essentially by a landscape around us, or by our life situation. That we only begin to marvel if there is something unusual 'out there' to be marvelled at. On this understanding, wonder might be provoked by a stunning sunset, a snow-capped mountain, or falling in love. But a grey day in the city, or 20 years of marriage to the same partner, will fail to provoke the same wonder.

It is an easy mistake to make. Most of us have had moments of heightened awareness, when we feel a quickening of the pulse, when the colours of nature seem all the more vivid, and birds seem to sing with a greater sweetness. It is easy to assume, therefore, that the wonder we are feeling is a by-product of our circumstances; and that, as our circumstances improve, so too will the wonder of life. However, this is patently not the case. On reflection, two flaws become clear.

Most of us know people who feel miserable and wonderless, whatever their circumstances. They could be in the most sublime natural beauty, with the most beautiful, intelligent partner, have beautiful children, a lovely home and untold wealth – and still feel bored and melancholic. Their patron saint might be Eeyore, the glum donkey in A. A. Milne's Winnie-the-Pooh stories, for whom every silver lining comes with a large, grey cloud attached. Maybe that is the mood some of us habitually find ourselves in. Such people know from bitter experience that a change of externals does little to affect the internal roots of their problem.

Secondly, this view condemns most of life to the spiral of unwonder. What about the 99 per cent of life when we are not staring open-mouthed at mountain peaks, or falling in love for the first time? Is this time, the majority of life, really to be written off as wonder-free? Even if we could sit daily contemplating the mountains, or falling in love repeatedly, we know full well that these experiences would not in themselves provoke the wonder we desire. We would become blasé about the most spectacular scenery, as routine made it familiar. We would lose the thrill of romance on passing ceaselessly from one partner to the next.

We must conclude, with the seventeenth-century English physician and essayist Sir Thomas Browne, that 'we carry with us the wonders we seek'.[9] Wonder is not something outside us. It is something we bring with us – wherever we are, whatever our circumstances.

The second mistake

Many recognize the error of making wonder dependent on our external circumstances, and agree with Sir Thomas Browne that wonder is carried within. However, they then fall into an equal and opposite error: writing off the external world, circumstances and other people altogether, focusing only on the inner life of the mind.

This is the assumption of many popular psychologists, New Agers, mystics, followers of Eastern religions and some Christian contemplatives. For such people, the only journey worth making is inwards. There, they say, is where the treasure is to be found: buried within ourselves is the key to spirituality, self-esteem, contentment and wonder.

The call to the inner journey sounds plausible and appealing. That is because it is half true. The way we feel inside really does colour the world we see. Contentment really is more to do with what is going on inside us than outside us. In a consumer culture which encourages us to root our identity and confidence in our possessions, the inner life holds out the promise of a deeper, wiser way. However, it is still only a half-truth. And half-truths made into full truths become untruths. This view, as a proposed total solution, is wrong for a couple of reasons.

The first is that it is over optimistic about what we might find as we dig. We are told we will find treasure within. What if there is no treasure to be found? What if we find we are digging into a hollow centre? Perhaps the self has been hollowed out by the gnawing of the pet 'If Only' we met in the last chapter. What if we find a dusty basement full of old junk from the past which we would rather forget? The inner journey might actually prove to be a journey from mild melancholy into deep depression and utter isolation.

Contemplatives talk of digging for treasure. And, to be sure, there is a rich heritage of Christian contemplation. But what if, as historic Christianity has always affirmed, the journey into the self might be not so much a descent into a gold mine as into quicksand? That descent seems less appealing. Going within ourselves does not by itself guarantee finding wonder.

The second reason why the inner journey alone is inadequate is because at the heart of wonder is the experience of being drawn beyond ourselves. It is about an awestruck encounter with 'otherness': with people who are different from us, with a world full of unexpected marvels, a God who draws us beyond the trivia of our own expectations. The journey deeper into the self might be a journey not into wonder but into solipsism – the idea that the only thing which is real and can be known is ourself.

The sixth sense

Somehow, we must hold apparently contradictory factors in tension. Wonder is triggered by an awestruck encounter with something or somebody beyond ourselves. But it is not dependent on those external circumstances. It is something we carry within us, but not something we should be focusing on unduly by introspection. Can we find an understanding of wonder which takes account of all this?

An answer is provided by the novelist D. H. Lawrence. Wonder, he says, is a sense, much like our senses of hearing, touch, taste, sight and smell. Lawrence's claim that the sense of wonder is 'the sixth sense'[10] is a helpful analogy. Like any other sense, wonder is something owned and carried by a person. It is not something located in the world around us, but in ourselves. Yet, at the same time, a sense is not something we focus on for its own sake. Rarely do we sit and examine our sense of sight or hearing for their own sakes. Nor should we. These are the means by which we relate to a world beyond ourselves.

Like any other sense, wonder has interior and exterior components. It is exterior to the extent that its purpose is to link us to the outside world; its focus is beyond the self. It is interior in that if the sense is paralysed or defective, our perceptions will be dulled or even shut down altogether.

Wonder is like our capacity to taste food. It depends both on the good functioning of our taste-buds and on having something tasty to put into our mouth. Those who look for wonder simply in external circumstances are like people who swallow fine foods without savouring the taste: they fail to realize that their own senses have a vital part to play in the experience. But those who claim that wonder is only to be found only within are like people telling us to taste our own tongues.

What sort of sense is wonder? Wonder is slightly different from each of our other five senses in that it is built on a combination of all the others. Wonder means using all our senses with a fresh acuteness. It means having a fresh curiosity about the world we encounter through these senses. We see, smell, hear, taste and touch it. We are filled with awe before the things we find, a sense of gratitude for them all, and a commitment to them. Wonder is a way of using our five senses, and of celebrating what they offer to our perception.

Senses reawakened

The spiral of wonder, then, begins in encounter. And encounter is about learning to freshen up the dullness of our senses. To some, this comes naturally: they seem spontaneously alive to the world and people around them. Some seem instinctively alert to encountering God in the world around them too. For most of us, however, the reawakening of our senses is a skill we need to learn.

Or perhaps learning is not the most helpful image. Christian writer Evelyn Underhill writes that wonder, like love, is not so much taught as caught, 'and to catch them we must be in an atmosphere where we are sure to find the germs'.[11] Perhaps we shall be helped not so much by learning principles of how to see, but by being around people who can see, and letting their enthusiasm and insight become infectious. This is a challenge both to the sort of people I surround myself with (do I mix with people who are wonder-filled, or with world-weary cynics?), and also to issues such as my reading and viewing habits (what kind of 'fuel' am I putting in my 'tank'?).

One group of people likely to infect us with the art of passionate encounter are artists: painters, poets, novelists, fabric designers, dressmakers, and so on. From them we may catch the germs of encountering afresh.

In 1871 the French artist Claude Monet, his wife Camille and their young son, Jean, moved into a house in the town of Argenteuil, close to the River Seine, north of Paris. Monet particularly liked to paint in the garden of their new house, and on the banks of the Seine. In the spring of the following year, he decided on an artistic experiment. He had always been fascinated above all else by light, particularly how one scene could appear quite different in different lights, depending on such circumstances as the time of day and the season. He chose a large clump of lilacs in one corner of his garden at Argenteuil, and painted them on two different occasions.

Lilacs in Dull Weather presents the scene in deep shadow, the colours of the blooms subdued. In *Lilacs in Sunshine*, on the other hand, the flowers form a bright, hazy blur of vivid pinks. Light falls on the grass beneath, and the shadows cast by the lilacs are crisper and more stark in their contrast than in the other painting. The two paintings are an experiment in seeing and encountering.

By the 1890s, Camille had died of tuberculosis, following the birth of their second son, Michel, and Monet and his sons were now living in Giverny, a small village in the countryside 40 miles from Paris. The name of Giverny would later become synonymous with Monet's paintings of his garden: the pool of water lilies, the ornamental bridge, the riots of vivid irises. In the years 1890 and 1891, he returned to his experiment in viewing the same scene under different conditions.

Monet went out into the fields around Giverny, painting farmers' haystacks at different times of day and in different lights. As with the lilacs of Argenteuil, his aim was to explore the effect different qualities of light had on a scene. In 15 paintings he captures, in extraordinary ways, fleeting moments of light and shade and the different combinations of colour evoked by those lights. *Haystacks, Late Summer, Evening Effect* is dominated by purples and long shadows, while *Haystacks, Late Summer, Morning Effect* radiates a bright, lemon-yellow radiance, and *Haystacks, Effect of Snow, Morning* is bathed in a pale, wintry light.

Between 1892 and 1894 Monet painted 40 pictures of the façade of Rouen Cathedral, from the same angle, in different lights. The artist even rented a room opposite the cathedral to study it more closely. Once again, the effect is to startle the viewer into reassessing the familiar. Monet paints to capture fleeting moments, the familiar transformed in countless ways by the effects of the season, the weather, the time of day. He paints to capture not just objects, but something we usually take for granted: our own capacity for seeing.

The poet Stéphane Mallarmé wrote to Monet in July 1890, 'You have so astounded me lately with your Haystacks that I catch myself looking at the fields through the prism of your paintings.'[12] This was precisely the point. Monet wanted to use his art to resensitize people into seeing the familiar with new eyes, to encounter afresh.

It is not only fine art and nature which have this capacity to resensitize. A meal well cooked and attractively presented can be a celebration of taste, colour and friendship. A well-designed dress can help us appreciate texture, form and the human body. The layout of a room and its choice of colours can enhance our moods. A well-crafted track of dance music can be a celebration of energy and harmony. A love poem can help us see our own relationships afresh. Science and mathematics in their own ways explore the order and chaos in both the universe and the human mind. The writings of contemporary popular novelists and poets help us see and celebrate the curious beauty of urban popular culture.

The point is this: to reawaken our senses to discover the extraordinariness of the ordinary, the miraculous in the mundane. The eyes of unwonder and wonder look out at the same scene. But what each sees is quite different.

GRATITUDE

The spiral of wonder rises through encounter with the world around us into an overwhelming feeling of gratitude for it all. This gratitude has two aspects: the joy of receiving a gift and a might-not-have-been factor.

The joy of receiving a gift

A characteristic of people filled with wonder is their sense that all they have is a gift. Gratitude is the opposite of taking things for granted. A well-worn maxim notes the difference between an optimist and a pessimist: while the optimist sees her glass half full, the pessimist sees his half empty. But wonder is more than optimism. Wonder looks in astonishment at the fluid in the glass and is inexpressibly grateful that such a thing exists at all.

Gratitude is made more acute when we realize that our gifts come from a giver whom we can thank. Think of it this way: I have a ball-point pen in a pot on my desk. If I had unthinkingly picked up that pen in the office and happened to bring it home, I would feel nothing special about it. Its origins would be impersonal. But if the pen had been a present from my daughter, who had saved up for weeks to buy it for my birthday, I should feel differently. It would be more than a pen: it would be an expression of love and appreciation, even if it wrote no better than the pen from the office. It is more precious because it has the character of a gift.

Or take another example. I spread plum jam on my breakfast toast. Usually this would come from the supermarket. But today I am eating a jam whose jar bears a label, handwritten by my father and carrying a date. The plums came from his own garden, and the jam was a gift to us. Now it may not taste very different from its factory-produced equivalent. But I eat every mouthful with greater appreciation, because this jam has the character of a personal gift. I know where it is from, and who has given it to me.

Extend this sense of gratitude as far as it will stretch,

into a whole philosophy of life, and the result is theism: belief in a personal God, who created all things and sustains all life. Theism really is the only approach to life which takes the idea of personal gratitude seriously.

The atheist can feel wonder (such as biologist Richard Dawkins, who finds the complexity of nature genuinely awe-inspiring), but it can only be the agreeable surprise of the person who finds a pen lying on the pavement. The pen writes well, but the joy the finder feels is at best an impersonal wonder. There is no gratitude at the heart of it, since the atheist doesn't believe that there's a Person to be grateful to. The pleasure of the atheist is quite unlike the gratitude I feel towards my daughter who gives me a pen as a gift.

Nor do other faith-systems account adequately for the personal gratitude I feel for the gift of my pen. The polytheist tells me wild stories about some disreputable and probably fictional characters long ago, who manufactured pens. The pantheist tells me that I and my pen are the same thing, did I but know it. The consumerist offers to sell me a new pen. The Freudian tells me I only like the pen because it reminds me of sex, and the Marxist tells me my pen is his. Only the theist tells me what my gratitude has already told me: that I have a daughter who gave me the pen as a gift, that my wonder is a response to a personal gift of love. My gratitude is not a wasted emotion.

Just one further observation on gratitude. We live in a culture which, since the eighteenth century, has been dominated by talk of 'rights'. Its clearest statement is in the famous Bill of Rights in the American constitution. This states that every person has certain inalienable rights, which the government and other people are powerless to infringe: to speak your mind, worship freely, and so on. Rights have become our standard yardstick for measuring personal freedoms.

However, despite its practical usefulness in a world where oppression is still rife, the whole business of rights sits uneasily with the rediscovery of wonder. The reason for this is that each begins from an opposite premise. Rights assume that the world owes us something, that there is a basic minimum we can demand from life. If this is not forthcoming, we have a right to protest.

Wonder is quite different. Wonder means being grateful and astonished that we have anything at all. To the eye of wonder, everything is a gift. To the wonder-filled theist, everything is a personal gift from a loved one. It is unlikely that people fixed on the idea that they have a right to their own life, to a certain minimum standard of living, to a life insured against excessive pain and suffering, will ever really grasp the gratitude which lies at the heart of wonder. I suspect this is what Francis of Assisi meant when he said, 'Blessed is he who expects nothing, for he shall enjoy everything.'

The idea that gratitude is intrinsic to our humanity is central to the Judaeo-Christian tradition. There, gratitude is the acknowledgement of a basic dependence and reverence towards God. We exist only because he gives life. The original sin in Eden was not eating forbidden fruit. That was merely a symptom. The primal sin was to believe the lie of the serpent that God was holding back from Adam and Eve something they deserved (Genesis 3.1). They had a choice: gratitude or ingratitude – and they chose ingratitude. That this is the primal sin is underlined by Paul, as he writes about the roots of human dilemma: 'For although they knew God, they neither glorified him as God nor gave thanks to him' (Romans 1.21).

The might-not-have-been factor

In my book *God, Sex and Generation X*, I recounted

38

my near-fatal car crash as I drove to work early one morning.[13] It took the experience of almost losing my life before I was struck by what should have been self-evident: I might never have existed in the first place. But I do. My own life is wonderful and precious, because it might never have been. It too is an unexpected gift.

The former dean of Westminster Abbey, Michael Mayne, writes well on this theme. In his book *This Sunrise of Wonder*, he writes from a cottage in the Alps:

> My subject is wonder, and my starting point is so obvious it often escapes us. It is me, sitting at a table looking out on the world. It is the fact that I exist, that there is anything at all. It is the *givenness* that astonishes: the fact that the mountains, the larch tree, the gentian, the jay, *exist*, and that someone called *me* is here to observe them.[14]

This might-not-have-been factor is the antidote to taking things for granted. It is stopping in our tracks to be amazed that the object in front of me is there at all. Here again, we are helped by the artist. To celebrate something by surrounding it with a frame or book, to interpret it in stone, wood or fabric, is to draw our attention to its existence. It is a challenge to our tendency to take things for granted. The artistic process is an act of gratitude that something *is*, rather than *is not*. To appreciate art and literature is to participate in the grateful, wondering gaze of the artist or writer.

COMMITMENT

The spiral of wonder moves me through encounter (when I learn to see things afresh) via gratitude (when I learn to appreciate them), to commitment. Here, I learn the art of passionate engagement with my life and surroundings.

Passionate engagement

To encounter something anew and find fresh gratitude for it can only have one consequence. We want to enjoy it, celebrate it, love it. To find ourselves marvelling over something (the place we are in, our possessions, the people around us, or whatever) fuels our commitment to it.

Passionate engagement helps keep our rampant 'If Onlys' in check. In the previous chapter we saw how these creatures grow into monsters as they are fed on fantasy. We need to stop allowing them to have their destructive way. Though they start as fun companions, they end by hollowing out our personalities and devastating our sense of wonder. The only way forward is extermination. The environment which is most toxic for the 'If Only' is passionate engagement.

Chasing one rabbit

My waistline was expanding. I was starting to get these jolly pokes in the stomach which say, 'Putting on weight, are we?' The final straw came when a relative pointedly told me of a church minister who grew so fat he no longer fitted into his pulpit.

I resolved to lose weight and get fitter, and my starting point was a shop selling training shoes. I stared open-mouthed at the hundreds of styles covering every wall. Some had reservoirs of air in the sole. Others looked like rubber models of our church plumbing system. One pair looked as if they could take you for a run, connect you to the Internet and microwave your supper at the same time.

I stood intimidated. Paralysed. An assistant asked me what I wanted. What *did* I want? I imagined the assistant creasing up, helpless with mirth at the naiveté of my answer, digging colleagues in the ribs: 'He wants trainers! Trainers! Everybody here wants trainers, mate. The question is . . . what sort of trainers?'

I studied the rows of ominous rubbery misshapes, resembling some evil breeding experiment on a Klingon starship. The choice was numbing. I had no idea where to start. I mumbled an apology and escaped, still trainerless.

In today's consumer culture, freedom to choose is all-important. Our culture loves to make choices, because the choices we make as we shop say something about who we are. My consumer choices – the magazines I read, the clothes I wear, the music I listen to – help to define my identity. Consumer choice is a central creed of our age, extending beyond trivia like trainers to the biggest issues of life. Today's adults choose not only their shampoos and fashions, but also their sexual and spiritual options, from a wide range on offer.

But unfettered choice can also be a commitment-inhibitor. We are always looking over our shoulder at the other options we could be taking. The result, so often, is that we defer passionate engagement with one particular path, lest it shut down other options. Yet in reality, it is precisely by shutting down other options and going all out for one that we will gain maximum happiness and wonder, whether in terms of relationships, faith, possessions or place.

There is an old saying: 'If you chase two rabbits, both will get away'. Our consumer culture believes it is doing us a favour by offering an unlimited number of rabbits to chase. The result is that we remain empty-handed. But chase one rabbit, and you might just catch it.

Committed to being me

We have noted how the end-point of having our mind taken over by a voracious 'If Only' is that we lose a desire to be ourselves. Only a bloated 'If Only' remains, telling us we should be somebody else, somewhere else, with different commitments from those we have made, at any other time than the present.

The restoration of wonder in each of us includes a fresh commitment to being oneself. It is not enough to learn appreciation and commitment to externals. This same process needs to extend to a fresh appreciation of me and a commitment to being me. This is not self-centredness or arrogance. It is a natural, healthy consequence of killing the 'If Only' which had no right to be eating up my wonder and contentment in the first place. From the standpoint of theism, I am learning to give thanks for the precious gift of myself, learning not to return that unique gift unopened, unappreciated.

WHATEVER THE CIRCUMSTANCES: PAUL

The main weapon in the armoury of motivational business speakers is the word 'attitude'. We cannot always change our circumstances, they tell us, but we can change our attitude. Positive thinking can achieve marvels in our personal and business life. Inspirational stories are told about leaders who succeeded because they had a winning attitude and were not defeated by circumstances.

So is the spiral of wonder just a variation on motivational psychology? A way of encouraging people to look on the bright side of life, whatever their situation, and learn to value what they have more? Certainly, attitude is important – more important than most people acknowledge. And yes, learning to count our blessings is a vital component of contentment. But is there more to it than this?

To answer that, we need to look at another life: that of a man who claimed to have found the secret to lasting happiness, wonder and gratitude. Around the year AD 61, a man from south-eastern Turkey found himself under house arrest in Rome. He was living in a rented house, which was guarded day and night to prevent his escape. And while he was in prison, he wrote a letter to a group of friends in the Macedonian city of Philippi.

It is a letter full of joy and contentment, despite the writer's difficult personal circumstances: he is under lock and key, and in just six or seven years, he will be put to death by the Roman authorities. Yet in this letter, the apostle Paul tells his friends in Philippi the secret of his contentment:

> I have learned to be content whatever the circumstances. I know what it is to be in need, and I know what it is to have plenty. I have learned the secret of being content in any and every situation, whether well fed or hungry, whether living in plenty or in want. (Philippians 4.11–12)

This passage is often held up as an example of attitude. Think positive, say the motivational speakers, and your life will be positive. Just look at Paul. However, closer inspection shows this to be a misreading of how Paul found his contented, wonder-filled outlook.

An educated man, Paul would have known that the idea of contentment whatever the circumstances had long been an ideal of classical thinkers. The Roman writer Seneca (echoing the Greek thinker Socrates) wrote, 'The happy man is content with his present lot, no matter what it is, and is reconciled to his circumstances'.[15] To a culture steeped in such writings, Paul proclaims he has found the key to a lifestyle which was the goal of the ancient philosophers.

But for Paul this key is no mere change of attitude through positive thinking. When he writes, 'I have learned . . .', he writes in the aorist tense, a form of the Greek verb which implies that his exciting insight came in a particular moment of revelation. Almost certainly, he is referring to the moment of his conversion, as a young man, some 25 or so years earlier. The reawakening of a sense of wonder and contentment for Paul did not come through studying classical philosophy or adopting the positive thinking of the motivational gurus of the classical world. What shook him out of his complacency was an experience so massive and traumatic that he came to understand it in terms of a rebirth.

Reborn into wonder

How did the faith into which Paul was converted enable him to 'carry with him the wonders he sought' (to quote Sir Thomas Browne again)? If we review the components of the spiral of wonder, and compare them with the claims of the faith embraced and developed by Paul, we discover that the match between the two is an extraordinarily close one. So close, in fact, that we might begin to suspect the similarity is more than coincidence.

We have seen that the surest way to rekindle wonder, even briefly, is to look the reality of death in the eye. A near-fatal crash or dangerous sport offers the edge of risk which leaves us panting with gratitude for the life we have. Paul's writing is permeated with the understanding that Christian believers have not merely flirted with death; they have actually gone through an experience of dying to an old self, emerging as a new, wonder-filled being (Romans 6.1–11; 2 Corinthians 5.17; Ephesians 2.1–5). Already in the present age, says Paul, we can begin to experience the wonder-filled reality of a future, resurrection life: the 'age to come' anticipated by centuries of Hebrew prophets.

For this reason, a key part of the symbolism of the water of baptism is death. At baptism, we celebrate a drowning. But from the death of an old self, we see a new being emerge, resurrected, from the waters.

We found that the spiral of wonder begins in a fresh encounter with life. This is neither dependent on circumstances, nor is it introspection. It involves a renewal of our own mind and senses, by which we perceive people and things. This is precisely what Paul tells his Christian friends living in another great city of his day, Ephesus. To be a Christian is 'to be made new in the attitude of your minds' (Ephesians 4.23). They are to see the world as if through new eyes.

We saw that a vital component of wonder is gratitude, and when gratitude is stretched out into an entire world-view, its name is theism. Paul was already a theist before he met Christ. But at his conversion, he came to an astounding realization: that the Jesus who appeared to him in his blinding vision shared the very nature of God himself (Ephesians 1.21–2; Philippians 2.6). This same Jesus was, so to speak, the human face of God. Paul's own gifts of life and rebirth, not to mention the gift of the whole created world, had a personal giver, whom he now personally encountered. Little wonder, then, that Paul finds himself constantly bursting into joyful thanks 'in all circumstances' (1 Thessalonians 5.16–18).

We also said that our consumer society is based on a fundamental untruth. For the key to wonder lies not in unlimited freedom of choice, but in commitment. In other words, in making the right choice, and pursuing those commitments with passion and joy. We chase just one rabbit in order to catch it. Paul would agree. In

45

the arena of faith, he celebrates a passionate monotheism (for example, Ephesians 4.4–6). In human relationships, he echoes the creation narrative of Genesis, and the words of Jesus, in celebrating passionate monogamy (Ephesians 5.31).

Finally, Paul has a basis for putting to death the voracious 'If Onlys' in his imagination. He knows himself to be a unique creation of God, reborn to fresh wonder in Christ, called to his own distinct vocation. This calling is not an easy one, but he pursues it with energetic single-mindedness. Nothing could be further from Paul's mind than a vague, restless desire to be somebody else, somewhere else, at another time. He is a man with a mission, a man fired by passion.

Ecclesiastes answered

We saw at the end of Chapter One a portrait of an elderly man, tired and visionless, living on the spiral of unwonder. His name is Solomon. We have also met another elderly man, passionate and visionary, living on the spiral of wonder. His name is Paul. The one dies jaded and bitter, with little hope left. The other dies a martyr, a witness to a blazing hope within him.

The contrasts between the two are dramatic. They are also instructive. Both are educated men from privileged backgrounds, and both love the pursuit of philosophical wisdom. Both have a rigorous training in theistic religion, and both have dramatic, awe-inspiring encounters with God as young adults. Both are born leaders and skilled communicators. Yet by old age, one is descending the spiral of unwonder, while the other is rising on the spiral of wonder. By now, some of the reasons for this should be clear:

- One has learned an attitude of gratitude and contentment, whatever his circumstances. The other has learned never to be grateful or contented: there is always one more nation to court, one more wife to marry, one more concubine to add to the harem, one more foreign god to add to the list.

- One enthusiastically chases a single rabbit. The other runs after a whole field of rabbits, only to find they all elude his grasp. One values commitment, the other choice.

- One discovers the wonder of his mind and senses renewed through spiritual rebirth. The other has convinced himself that there is 'nothing new under the sun' (Ecclesiastes 1.9). The result is that one has a vision of the world which is alive and brimfull of meaning, where the other concludes it is meaningless (Ecclesiastes 1 and 2). While one sustains a sense of hope, the other finds he has drifted into hopelessness, and can see no way back.

- One talks of standing in awe of God (Ecclesiastes 5.7), but his words have a lethargic and hollow ring, since he has clearly chosen to turn his back on the God he previously encountered face to face. The other falls physically to the ground, filled with terror, struck down by awe in the presence of God (Acts 9), and never loses that sense of awe. Everything he does is coloured by a sense of the ever-present, personal reality of God and his purposes for his life and the unfolding story of the universe.

We have begun to see how the Bible offers some insights into lives lived on the spirals of wonder and unwonder. In the next three chapters we shall use the two spirals, and a range of biblical snapshots, to explore how we might begin to restore wonder in three areas: where we live, the present moment, and the life of faith.

CHAPTER THREE

THE WONDER
OF HERE

> We don't see things as they are, we see them as we
> are.
>
> (Anaïs Nin)

INDIFFERENCE, FANTASY, WITHDRAWAL

I recently attended one of those parties where elegant people sip drinks and make small-talk. The most depressing feature of such parties is that you always meet Mr Shoulderman. He turns up without fail. Some time during the evening, your host brings him over and introduces him. For the first few seconds, he smiles and chats amiably. But before long it becomes harder to catch his eye. You realize he is constantly looking over your shoulder, surveying the room. He is looking to see if there is somebody more interesting, influential or attractive than you.

Soon his gaze is directed almost constantly over that shoulder, scanning the room for more promising talent. You offer your reflections on your children's schooling and the weather. He responds with bored monosyllables and lethargic grunts. After some minutes of this, you long to snap your fingers, attract his attention, and scream, 'Listen! Just come out with it and tell me you find me boring. You've spent the last ten minutes eyeing up everybody else in the room, and not paying the slightest attention to me!' But you have been too well brought up. You don't want to make a scene. So you tell him how good it has been to meet him, and politely slip off to refill your glass.

We dread these meetings with Mr Shoulderman, because his inattention leaves us feeling dull and second-rate. Yet the way Mr Shoulderman treats us in conversation is the way many of us treat the place we live: repeatedly looking over its shoulder, scanning for new talent.

Home on the spiral of unwonder

I grew up in the small Warwickshire town of Kenilworth. Like most teenagers in the town during the 1970s, I found Kenilworth dull. I remember a phone-in poll on national radio to find the most boring town in Britain. The winner was Grantham, but it was a close-run thing. I think we came second. It gave us Kenilworth teenagers a curious sort of pride to know that our town was not only boring. It was award-winningly boring.

This was not how tourists thought of our town. They came in droves to see the ruins of Kenilworth Castle. Begun under Norman rule, the castle reached the height of its glory in Elizabethan times. In 1575, Queen Elizabeth I was entertained there in great style by Robert Dudley, Earl of Leicester. Later, as a centre of royalist sympathies, it was a prime target for the Parliamentary forces in the English Civil War and was left in ruins. The town was the subject of a historical novel by Sir Walter Scott: *Kenilworth*, published in 1821.

None of this extraordinary history mattered as I was growing up. What use is a medieval castle to a teenager who wants bowling alleys and rock concerts?

The spiral of unwonder begins in indifference. The

49

place I live might be communicating any amount of information to me, inviting me to engage with it, but my eyes glaze over and I lose interest. This indifference may be a consequence of boredom: I see the same streets, the same shops, the same public buildings day after day, and familiarity breeds lethargy. After living here many years, these things hold no more mystery. Nothing startles me or astonishes me.

The traditional cause of indifference is overfamiliarity. However, the opposite can also be true: many people now are so mobile that they have no time to put down roots in an area. As recently as 150 years ago, 98 per cent of the people in the world lived in rural areas. Now, for the first time ever, over half live in cities.[1] A characteristic of today's urban life is that people are less settled in one place, usually due to work pressures. In my own north London parish, most residents are young adults in rented flats. They live here for a year or two before moving on. Even while they are here, the chances are that they work in a different part of London, socialize in another and sometimes attend church in yet another. Few have seen their next-door neighbour. Few feel any sense of belonging in this area, or any commitment to it. Factors such as good public transport outweigh any attachment to the area itself.

The indifference we feel soon turns to fantasies of escape. We look over the shoulder of the place before us, convinced that anywhere else would be preferable. The man in Sutton Coldfield craves the ocean; the suburban housewife dreams of the fashion stores and theatres of the city. The professor from the Mid-West dreams of the cultured cities of Europe; the teenager in the historic town yearns for cheap jeans and MTV.

Fantasy fuels withdrawal. We no longer pay attention to where we are. We pass through it without noticing. We prefer the virtual communities of the Internet or substitute communities on TV. We do to the place where we live what Mr Shoulderman does to us at parties: grudgingly acknowledging our existence, barely stifling the yawns, waiting for something better to come along. Whatever the address on our mail, the real place many of us live is on the spiral of unwonder.

Home on the spiral of wonder

Until Mr Shoulderman learns to give the guest before him his undivided attention, he will never find anyone in the room who is more interesting, now or at any future party. He will be perpetually condemned to acting out the same restless ritual.

The key to restoring the wonder of place is learning to see with new eyes, to discover how to stop taking our neighbourhood and community for granted. Unless we learn this art of seeing and appreciating afresh, we will only ever see places from the vantage point of a slow descent down the spiral of unwonder. We may move from city to country to suburbs; we can live at home or abroad; we may become sightseers at the most spectacular sites in the world; but we will never experience the full wonder of place until we learn to see properly. And that process begins in encounter.

ENCOUNTER

Adventure begins on our own doorstep. But few of us realize that, since few of us look at our doorstep. We dream of exotic travel, we fantasize of owning a new home in a chic district, because most of us still believe, deep down, that our level of wonder depends on our environment and our circumstances. But it doesn't. As we found in the last chapter, wonder is a way of seeing. It is our own capacity for engaging passionately with our environment and circumstances, whatever they

51

are. Wonder is not a place we travel to. It is something we carry with us.

Take Kenilworth Castle. What kind of person might look at the majestic ruins of the castle with a maximum sense of wonder? Not the local teenager. His familiarity has dulled his capacity to see it afresh. What about a casual sightseer, on a whistle-stop tour of central England? He would see it, all right. But he would see just another historical curiosity, sandwiched between the grander (and less ruined) Warwick Castle in the morning, and Stratford-on-Avon that evening.

But now meet Jane. She is a student of British history, who lives in Portland, Oregon. Her specialist subject is Elizabethan England. She has read all about the Earl of Leicester's gardens at Kenilworth: how one of the castle walls was the backdrop to a raised grassy terrace, 10 feet high and 12 feet wide, bearing exquisite white stone ornaments on posts: heraldic beasts, obelisks, balls.[2] Jane has read about the moat which once surrounded Kenilworth Castle, and the feasting and bear-baiting which accompanied the first Queen Elizabeth's visit. She has had her imagination fired by reading Scott's novel.

For years she has dreamed of visiting the places she has read about. So when she can afford the flight to England, her destination is Kenilworth. She travels with the eagerness and passion of a pilgrim: going halfway round the world to see what to somebody else is a small town and a heap of ruins. When she finally enters the castle grounds, she steps with the tread of a pilgrim who knows herself to be walking on holy ground. She looks not with the dulled eyes of the local teenager, or the speedy and superficial eye of the sightseer, but the intense gaze of the pilgrim, for whom every ancient stone becomes an object of amazement.

To encounter a place afresh, I must see it through the eyes of a passionate outsider. To see my own neighbourhood afresh, it must become a place of pilgrimage. I need to become a pilgrim in my own parish.

Pilgrim in her parish

We have suggested that a wonder-filled way of seeing is not so much taught as caught, and that the most infectious people to be around are artists and writers. One author who embodies this fresh clarity of vision is the American essayist, Annie Dillard.

To read Dillard is to eavesdrop on a fascinating interior conversation. We follow one woman's passionate attempts to encounter the world around her and make sense of it all – with the sharp, questioning eye of faith. She writes in a dense and poetic style which resists any attempts at skip-reading and paraphrase. Dillard is not an easy writer, but writes exquisitely. Her book *Pilgrim at Tinker Creek* won the Pulitzer Prize for nonfiction. In it, she writes of her time living in a valley in Virginia's Blue Ridge Mountains, close to the creek of the book's title.

She reflects how the heart of wonder lies in looking beyond the immediate and obvious:

> It's all a matter of keeping my eyes open. Nature is like one of those line drawings of a tree that are puzzles for children: Can you find hidden in the leaves a duck, a house, a boy, a bucket, a zebra and a boot? Specialists can find the most incredibly hidden things.[3]

Like Monet, Annie Dillard is minutely sensitive to the effects of light on a scene:

As I walked along the grassy edge of the island, I got better and better at seeing frogs both in and out of the water. I learned to recognise, slowing down, the difference in texture of the light reflected from mudbank, water, grass or frog.[4]

Or again:

The sun in the west illuminates the ground, the mountains, and especially the bare branches of trees, so that everywhere silver trees cut into the black sky like a photographer's negative of a landscape ... Fifteen minutes later another darkness is coming overhead from the northwest; and it's here. Everything is drained of its light as if sucked. Only at the horizon do inky mountains give way to distant, lighted mountains – lighted not by direct illumination but rather paled by glowing sheets of mist hung before them.[5]

The effect of spending time with an ecstatic such as Annie Dillard is that we start to become 'infected' too: our own capacity to see our own environment starts to become resensitized.

Pilgrim in my parish

This art of seeing your environment with fresh eyes might sound relatively easy for somebody living in the scenic beauty of Virginia, or near the ruin of a medieval castle (although, as we have found, wonder lies more in the seeing than the thing seen). But what about all the drab places which can surely inspire no wonder at all? Let's take a closer look at two of the least promising 'parishes' imaginable. One is a run-down inner-city area, the other a ramshackle collection of huts on a disused army base.

First, the inner-city parish. This area is a former

red-light district, where a few prostitutes are still active. Situated on the edge of three separate London boroughs, this place has been neglected by all three down the years. In many parts it still has an abandoned feel to it. It has been associated with some high-profile murders and abductions and, in recent memory, a woman's dead body was found in the churchyard. The area is best known for its summer rock festivals in the park, when litter in local streets is ankle deep. A large gang of alcoholics sprawls outside the main entrance to the park in all weathers.

I know all this, because it is where I and my family live at the time of writing. It is my parish: Finsbury Park, north London. At first glance, Finsbury Park does not have a great deal going for it. But then I started to look more closely. That involved reading up on local history, beginning to talk to local people, reading census data for the area and – most of all – keeping my eyes open and looking intently. Here are a few of the things I found.

When Victorian merchant bankers moved to the countryside north of London, they named the area Finsbury Park, after Finsbury in the City of London. But the older name for the area had been Brownswood Park, thought to be derived from Roger le Brun, a Norman priest. When they built the old St John's Church (forerunner of my own modern building) in 1874, they used a design which had first been submitted for Cork Cathedral in Ireland.

The Sainsbury's supermarket where I shop was built on the site where Billy Graham held his famous 1954 Haringey Crusade, and helped shape a whole generation of British Christianity. In 1973 the rock musical *Lonesome Stone* was performed at the local Rainbow Theatre. This marked the arrival of America's Jesus Movement and Christian rock music in the UK.

When the Beatles played the Rainbow, Finsbury Park, in the early 1960s they lodged in a house in Queen's Drive, opposite my church. I recently led a funeral for a family who had peered from their bedroom window at the young Paul McCartney and John Lennon, playing snooker in a back room.

A local privet bush is not the shapeless mess it first appears. If you stand back a few paces, you will see that it has been cut into the shape of a large, smiling face, with a big sprout of hair on top. It makes me smile every time I walk past it.

This area is amazingly multi-ethnic. One Sunday morning we surveyed the members of our little church, and found we came from over 20 countries. When we have a church lunch, the food is mostly Caribbean and African. On Sunday mornings we get a small foretaste of the day when people from every nation, tribe, people and language will stand together before the throne of God.

My first hero, T Rex vocalist Marc Bolan, came from nearby Stoke Newington. The local library still has his leather hat on display. They also have the tombstone of another one-time local resident, *Robinson Crusoe* author Daniel Defoe.

Today I delivered a letter to a parishioner, and my two young children came with me. As we passed a bush growing through a broken wall, we saw on its leaves a number of hairy caterpillars, striped in black and bright yellow. 'Look!' said my daughter, 'They're all wearing bee-suits!'

On a clear night you can look from our lounge window and see masses of tiny lights, as far away as Canary Wharf in London's Docklands. It makes you think about the lives of all those different people, living in all those lit rooms.

Our church is still surrounded by the original

Victorian stone wall from the old church. One of the stones in the wall contains a tiny, perfectly-preserved fossil of a seashell.

In bright sunlight, the dull concrete tower-blocks behind our house shine like sheer, white cliffs. At sunset, they glow with vivid crimsons and mauves.

Wild poppies have started growing in the cracks between the paving slabs outside our back door.

Pilgrim on a Norfolk beach

Another example of a place which seems less than wonderful at first glance is a grey strip of land called Snettisham beach, set on England's windswept west Norfolk coast. Never a sandy beach, much of it was concreted over during the last war, and turned into an army barracks and firing-range. These days, a chaotic jumble of huts can be seen there, some with paintwork peeling and windowsills rotting. It is far from the sun-baked, golden-sanded, palm-lined beach of holiday brochures.

I know about Snettisham because it is where my in-laws live. My father-in law, Nigel Holmes, spent his working life as a church minister. A few years ago, he retired with his wife to a small cottage on Snettisham beach. When he was approached by a publisher to write a book of reflections for Lent, he decided to explore the theme of how we encounter God in our daily lives. The resulting book is called *Looking For God*, and contains reflections on where God is to be found.[6] Where he starts, however, is not with grand theological abstractions, but right there, on the shingle beach outside his door.

Nigel delves into local history and meets local people. He finds out, among other facts, that in the 1900s the beach was Queen Alexandra's personal retreat, and that the area reminded her of her childhood near

Copenhagen. He tells how she had a bungalow built on the beach from the local stone. On the roof-ridge she had engraved, in Latin, words from Psalm 127: 'Unless the Lord builds the house, its builders labour in vain'.

At the end of the chapter, in a section of questions for further reflection, he asks possibly the most eccentric question in any Christian study book: 'If you had been Queen Alexandra, aged 60, what would you have carved on the ridge over your beach bungalow?'[7] Further back in history, he encounters the obscure eighth-century East Anglian saint, St Guthlac, and his battles against the forces of evil amid the wild waterlands of the Wash.

But most of his 'research' was done simply by looking and by engaging with what he could see, using what Wordsworth calls a 'baptized imagination'. He looks intently at the wild, bleak beauty of the place: the flotsam on the beach, the village church, the marshland, the tides and the endless variety of sea birds. Each becomes a thing of wonder in itself, and a window through which the eternal is glimpsed:

Down on the beach, February is the cruellest month. One's reserves have been drained, and Spring's renewal is only close enough to be tantalising. One good day gives way to a chill grey wind, and the feeling of being cheated is hard to resist. All the same, the sounds, if not the feeling of Spring, are there to hold onto, an embryonic language telling us to believe in what we cannot as yet see. The language of birds, in the dawn chorus, which will soon be gathering to a crescendo as day by day March strides on towards the equinox, prepares them for the activity of Spring. Flowers, too, have a language, expressed in their tapestry of colour, preparing them for summer fruitfulness – daffodils and bluebells in the gardens, followed by a carpet of mauve sea rocket and delicate yellow-horned poppy...For us, the language of Christian hope prepares us for Easter.[8]

Let's not misunderstand the value of such meditations. The point is not that we become literary tourists, undertaking an 'Annie Dillard Tour of Virginia' or a 'Nigel Holmes Tour of Norfolk Beaches'. The point is that each of us is already living in that place of wonder. Even if where we live is wilderness. There is a long spiritual tradition of retreating or being sent into the wilderness, and finding there not a place of barrenness, but of testing, encounter and growth: witness the lives of Hagar (Genesis 16), Moses and the people of Israel (from Exodus 13 to the end of Deuteronomy), David (1 Samuel 23–24), John the Baptist (Luke 1.80; 3.1, 2) and Jesus (Matthew 4.1–11).[9]

The place you are in is full of wonders, even if that place is wilderness. Open your eyes wide enough, look for long enough, and you will see.

GRATITUDE

If the first stage of living on the spiral of wonder is encountering where you are, the second is gratitude for it. We have seen how gratitude includes a might-not-have-been factor. In terms of finding the wonder of place, this means learning to appreciate the fact that such a place is there at all, learning to value its uniqueness.

Annie Dillard's ecstatic response to the beauty of Tinker Creek was not an inevitable response. *Pilgrim at Tinker Creek* is the result of the coming together of a number of factors: an intense gaze, a baptized imagination, and her unique setting. Imagine a very different Annie Dillard writing a postcard home from the same scene, this time an Annie Dillard who looked at her environment the way most of us look at ours:

Tinker Creek
Virginia

Dear Mother,

It is now my second day here at Tinker Creek. Weather still no better. Frogs still keeping me awake at night. Evenings boring. Why didn't the Finkelsteins ever get a TV connected? Scenery pleasant. Yesterday I saw a giant waterbug eating a frog. Yuck! Can't wait to get back to civilization.

Your loving daughter,

Annie

Or imagine Nigel Holmes sitting in his cottage on Snettisham beach, wishing he could be in a very different type of seaside resort: longing for the amusement arcades, night clubs and bingo halls of Blackpool, or the palm trees and deep blue seas of the Indian Ocean. As it is, Nigel looks intently at the windswept Norfolk coast and finds signs of the presence of God. His eye could easily have stopped at the gull-guano on his windscreen.

The distinctive charm of Snettisham is its wild, windswept quality. To appreciate Snettisham, you need to grow to love it for what is there: marshes and gravel pits, the wide horizon, the bracing winds, the tides, the hundreds of species of birds. Such a place might never have existed, anywhere in the world. But it does. You find wonder in Snettisham by being grateful for what it is, not by longing for what it could never be.

Equally, it would be crazy for me to sit amid the

tower-blocks of Finsbury Park, wishing I were in Snettisham or rural Virginia. Finsbury Park has many wonders, but they are not the wonders of tides or mountain walks. They are the wonders of being near the heart of a busy metropolis, access to exotic foods, proximity to theatres, the Arsenal football ground, music festivals, the privilege of having people from every place on the globe living in the same street.

There might never have been such a place as Finsbury Park, with its unique history and multicultural mix. There is nowhere else like it in the world. But here it is. And I, together with my neighbours, have the privilege of living here. Like the apostle Paul, we need to learn to give thanks at all times and in all circumstances. But especially for where we are right now.

Celtic gratitude

'B-grade' wonder is full of the wonder of place, but has nobody to thank for it. 'A-grade' wonder directs its thanks towards God as the giver of such generous, gratuitous diversity. To be infected by this kind of gratitude, the best company to keep is that of the ancient Celtic Christians, who understood well how to be pilgrims in their own parish.

An ancient Irish poem echoes what we have discovered: that wonder and insight do not lie in a restless longing for the unattainable. They are always on our own doorstep:

To go to Rome
Is much of trouble, little of profit;
The King whom thou seekest here,
Unless thou bring Him with thee, thou wilt not find.[10]

The world of these men and women was the mountains, lakes and villages of Ireland, Scotland and Wales, and islands such as Iona, Aran and Lindisfarne.

A contemporary writer on Celtic Christianity, Esther de Waal, notes how the Celtic saints were skilled at seeing their own environment, and allowing it to speak to them of the Creator: 'These early Celtic scribes and hermits lived, by the destiny of their dedication to a life of prayer and solitude, in places of great beauty, and they brought to their environment eyes washed miraculously clear by continual contemplation.'[11]

Back in the ninth century, Irish monks would routinely copy out the works of a Latin grammarian called Priscian. In the margin of one such manuscript, a monk has written the following poem:

> A hedge of trees surrounds me, a blackbird's lay
>   sings to me, praise I shall not conceal,
> Above my lined book the trilling of the birds
>   sings to me.
> A clear-voiced cuckoo sings to me in a grey cloak
>   from the tops of bushes,
> May the Lord save me from Judgement; well do
>   I write under the greenwood.[12]

An air of gratitude breathes through these ancient Celtic poems and prayers:

> Thanks be to Thee, Jesu Christ,
> For the many gifts Thou hast bestowed on me,
> Each day and night, each sea and land,
> Each weather fair, each calm, each wild.[13]

One of the main characteristics of Celtic spirituality is its earthiness and embeddedness in daily life. In the late nineteenth century a Scotsman by the name of Alexander Carmichael worked for the Scottish Customs and Excise Department. This gave him many opportunities to visit the Western Highlands and the Outer Hebrides (or Western Isles) off north-west Scotland. During these visits he collected songs, prayers, poems and stories which had been handed down the generations. A Gaelic speaker, he initially published his collection in two volumes in 1900, under the title, *Carmina Gadelica: Hymns and Incantations*. The *Carmina* contains a range of moving prayers and songs which were still in everyday use for all occasions of life: birth and death, fishing and milking, kindling the fire, and journeys.[14]

There is a line of descent from the Celtic Christians to contemporary writers such as Annie Dillard. It would, however, be as easy to misunderstand the value of the Celtic saints as that of a writer such as Dillard. We can read their writings as eloquent poems and prayers. We can grow misty eyed over their evocations of a simpler age, when people lived closer to nature. But this would be missing the point. The real gift of the Celts is to teach us a way of looking: intently, and soaked in gratitude. They teach us to look not so much at the places where *they* were, but at the place where *we* are, be that a Hebridean croft, or a suburb of Birmingham.

Like Moses faced with the awesome presence of God in the burning bush (Exodus 3), we need to discover that the place we are standing right now is holy ground. It is both a place unique in itself, and a place where we can encounter God. Rather than taking our neighbourhood for granted, we should be taking off our shoes in awe and reverence.

Finding gratitude and God in the city

For all their poems and songs, the Celtic Christians were the opposite of romantic escapists. They were grateful realists, who happened to eke out their harsh lives among spectacular natural beauty. But is it even possible to find gratitude and signs of the presence of God in the city or suburbs? Down the centuries, it is true that most Christian contemplatives have had their sights on nature. But there is also a strong tradition of urban spirituality, of people whose heart is in the city and who meet with God there. It is a tradition which includes biblical forebears such as Joseph, Nehemiah, Jeremiah and Daniel. Its mentor is the apostle Paul, who lived in the biggest, busiest urban centres of the Roman empire. The earliest churches began in an almost entirely urban setting.

The Reformation of the sixteenth century was centred mainly in the cities, the big cultural and economic centres of early modern Europe, and the origins of the Pentecostal movement in the early twentieth century were in downtown Los Angeles. There is a strong Christian precedent for urban wonder.

One of the most helpful Christian books of recent years is *God at the End of the Century*, by David Spriggs.[15] Spriggs is a Baptist minister, currently working for The Bible Society. His book essentially transplants a Celtic approach to spirituality into an urban setting, offering guidance on becoming an urban contemplative, teaching us how to learn gratitude for our busy, built-up surroundings, and allowing God to 'speak' to us through them.

His meditations are sparked by close observation of his own surroundings: looking out over his neighbour's house and washing-line, standing on a motorway bridge, looking at a radio, even seeing rubbish lying in the gutter:

> It was the Coke can that gained my attention . . . I could have been angry that some person uncaring about the environment had not only cluttered the gutter, giving a sense of untidiness and lack of care,

but had also added an extra risk, for if someone should fall they could cut themselves on the now exposed edge of the can...and so I might have thought about the way sin works...I could also have concentrated on the way a now ugly object had been the vehicle of refreshment on a hot summer's day, of the contrast between the content and the container.[16]

Instead, he sees in the can an object of care and skill in design and manufacture, now distorted and disregarded. This, in turn, provokes reflections on the lot of elderly people in urban society, so often cast off and neglected:

No longer could I see an object in the gutter, but rather a challenge to care for people and place them in God's perspectives. There were many other tatters that lay there too, such as a cigarette stub, a few leaves, scraps of paper...each could have spoken to me of God's truth. What will you see?[17]

COMMITMENT

When we are living on the spiral of wonder, encounter fuels gratitude, which in turn generates commitment. G. K. Chesterton writes eloquently about the necessity of passionate commitment to a place in order to find wonder there. In his 1908 classic, *Orthodoxy*, he writes with characteristic wonder about Pimlico, an area of London close to the Thames. In Chesterton's day Pimlico was a district of unfashionable residential estates. But, he writes:

If there arose a man who loved Pimlico, then Pimlico would rise into ivory towers and golden pinnacles; Pimlico would attire herself as a woman does when she is loved . . . If men loved Pimlico as mothers love children, arbitrarily, because it is *theirs*, Pimlico in a year or two might be fairer than Florence. Some readers will say that this is a mere fantasy. I answer that this is the actual history of mankind ... Men did not love Rome because she was great. She was great because they had loved her.[18]

How do we love the place we are in? By commitment to it, and by killing the 'If Onlys' rampaging in our imagination. When an 'If Only' rears its head and tells us that the place we are is not worth loving, that we should be happier if only we were in Tahiti or Iona, Venice or Montana, the 'If Only' must be firmly silenced because it is lying. We carry with us the wonder we seek.

This is not to say that we should never move home. A move can be necessary, desirable and sometimes inevitable. But it is to say that since we are where we are, at least for now, we might as well discover the hidden wonders of the place. If we feel indifference towards it, fantasize about leaving it, and withdraw from it, we merely accelerate the spiral of unwonder.

In the year 597 BC, the Hebrew prophet Jeremiah wrote a letter. It was written at a time of extreme violence and political uncertainty. He wrote to the people of Israel, who, eight years before, had been carried off into forced exile to the city of Babylon, the city whose name recurs in the Bible as a byword for evil. We might expect the letter to recommend civil disobedience, escape or insurrection. In fact, the message from God which Jeremiah passed on to the surviving exiles is astonishing:

Build houses and settle down; plant gardens and eat what they produce. Marry and have sons and daughters; find wives for your sons and give your daughters in marriage, so that they too may have sons and

66

daughters. Increase in number there; do not decrease. Also, seek the peace and prosperity of the city to which I have carried you into exile. Pray to the LORD for it, because if it prospers, you too will prosper. (Jeremiah 29.5–7)

Even people who live in the heart of an evil empire are to live on the spiral of wonder. We are called to seek the peace and prosperity of the most unlikely places.

Seeking the peace and prosperity of the city

The London borough where I live has long been a byword for failure. Hackney's schools are often near the bottom of the league tables. Our councillors have been notorious locally for petty political point-scoring and time-wasting. Council meetings have often degenerated into squalid slanging matches, and councillors are famous for blaming everybody but themselves for the borough's problems. The English language even has a word, 'hackneyed', which means dull or commonplace. The origins of these derogatory associations lie in the fourteenth century, when Hackney was a place where horses were raised: a 'hackneyed' horse meant a weak, hired horse. Later, the word was associated with 'hackney carriages', because of their drab and uniform appearance.

Eventually Hackney church leaders decided enough was enough. We could see local elections looming on the horizon, and the prospect of the same councillors being re-elected filled us with horror. Together, we drew up a hard-hitting document, *A Time to Speak*, which accused our elected councillors of poor political decision-making, leading to inadequate provision of services, infighting, failing to address the problems of Hackney's schools, and of constantly passing the buck.

It called for an overhaul of politics in the borough,

67

rooting out corruption, and demanded that councillors speak less and listen more. But the document not only criticized the council. It repented of our churches' indifference to local politics in the past, urged believers to pray for local politicians, to live as good neighbours and – where possible – support positive council initiatives.

On the eve of the local elections, *A Time to Speak* was distributed to candidates. Prayer meetings were held at the town hall, to ask for God's forgiveness for both church and council failings, and to pray for the elections. Over 200 of us attended. To be frank, most of us had become so disillusioned with the culture of local government that we didn't raise our hopes too high. At least, we reflected, it had brought the churches together with a common cause.

We could hardly believe what happened next. The council leader, whom many had blamed (rightly or wrongly) for the ills of Hackney local government, was soundly defeated by a Green Party candidate. The next thing we knew, the new Green councillor approached the churches with a view to making the ethical principles we had suggested the foundation document for the newly elected council.

A revised document was drawn up, called *A New Trust*. This distilled in ten statements a vision of a new council, where all parties would work honestly for the people of Hackney and avoid the failings of the past. At the first meeting of the new council, all four parties unanimously agreed the document. Hackney council now has at the heart of its life and work a robust statement of ethical principles, drawn up by the local churches. Jewish and Muslim leaders, who share our concerns, gave it their support too.

A declaration is only words on paper. But it is a start. And it shows that it really is possible to encounter the place you live, feel grateful for it, and be committed enough to work for its peace and prosperity. It is possible to begin to live on the spiral of wonder. Even in unpromising places.

CHAPTER FOUR

THE WONDER
OF NOW

Write it on your heart that every day is the best day
of the year.

(Ralph Waldo Emerson)

The time traveller

In 1895 a young English writer published his first
novel. With *The Time Machine*, H. G. Wells tackled a
theme that was to grip the imaginations of novelists
and film-makers to our own day: time travel. In Wells's
novel the hero, known as the Time Traveller, travels
only forward in time. And he is essentially a vehicle
for exploring the author's passion for Darwinism. As he
travels to the distant future, he witnesses humanity's
evolution into two distinct species: Eloi (peaceful
creatures, who live above ground) and Morlocks (ugly,
subterranean beings who prey on them). It is a bleak
vision, laden with comment on the belief and culture
of late Victorian England.

By 1985, time travel had lightened up and reached a
mass audience. In Robert Zemeckis's *Back to the
Future* movies, Marty McFly (Michael J. Fox) travels in
a souped-up DeLorean sports car to the past and future.
All he has to do is set the car's time clock to the year
he chooses.

In the last chapter we said that most of us routinely

fail to 'see' the place we are in. It is as if we look over the shoulder of our current surroundings, scanning the scene for more promising prospects. This escapism means indifference to where we are, fantasies of escape, and emotional withdrawal from it. We then began to ask how seeing the same *place* from the spiral of wonder might affect our appreciation of it. In this chapter, we consider what the two spirals might look like applied to *time*.

INDIFFERENCE, FANTASY, WITHDRAWAL

Each of us comes with a built-in time-travel control as powerful as that inside Marty McFly's DeLorean, which enables us to make our home in the past, present or future. How we set that control has a profound effect on our level of wonder. Leave it set permanently for travel to past or future, and you are not simply heading for another era. You are heading for trouble.

Wonder, we have seen, grows from encounter with our present surroundings, gratitude for them and commitment to them. In the same way, it also grows from encounter with, gratitude for and commitment to the present moment.

Not realizing this, many people stubbornly refuse to encounter the present. They find refuge in the past, or are held prisoner by it. They escape into a real or imagined future. They do anything but find wonder and contentment in the present. The spiral of unwonder involves becoming indifferent to today, having fantasies of escape from it, and withdrawing from it. Here are some of the ways we set our time-travel controls to past or future.

Nostalgia
Many people escape the demands of the present by

idealizing a period from their own past. For some, this period is childhood. They look back in fondness on a simpler time of life, before adult cares began to sap their joy and spontaneity. Christian writer Cornelius Plantinga recalls watching the TV show *Candid Camera*. On one programme a middle-aged trucker was asked what age he would most like to be:

> There was a silence for a while as the trucker con-templated the question. What was he thinking? Was he hankering for age 65 and retirement . . . or was he yearning for age 18 and the chance to go back and take some turn he had missed?
>
> Finally he turned to the interviewer and said that if it was up to him he'd like to be three. Three? why three? the interviewer wanted to know. 'Well', said the trucker, 'when you're three you don't have any responsibilities.'[1]

Many, like that trucker, set their time-travel control to early childhood, convinced that this is where wonder lies.

For others, that golden age is student life. My wife and I returned to our old college for a dinner, some years after we had left. We sat near people who had been students around the same time as us. As they talked, it became clear that for many of them, student days were the only time they had felt fully alive. They looked back to a golden age of freedom, between the limitations of childhood and the grind of adulthood.

The same people I remembered as exuberant, cre-ative people at 20 had, in just four or five years, become serious-minded, world-weary and jaded. The only time their eyes briefly lit up was when they remembered student pranks, punt parties and relationships.

Others' golden time is a moment of achievement or potential: the singer reliving her brief spell of fame, the ageing footballer recalling his peak form. Both are choosing not to live in the present and explore the full potential of *now*. Others may not consciously idealize a particular past time, but certain things about them – the way they dress or speak, their social life, the potions on the dresser – say quite clearly that they are pining for lost youth.

The same dynamic can operate in organizations such as churches. Whole congregations of time travellers fondly set their dials to the blessing of another era. For some this might be a glorious awakening in 1904. For others it is the heady days of 1994 and the 'Toronto blessing'. And for others, the great preaching of Pastor Suchandsuch, three decades ago. For another type of church the golden era might be the glory days when all churches used a common pattern of worship, such as the Latin Mass or the Book of Common Prayer. For others it is the days before modern Bible translations.

The result of such time travel is that people tend to write off the present. The present minister is never as good as the old one; the new services and Bibles can never recapture the poetry of the old; today's congregation doesn't have the spiritual passion of the one in 1904; on it goes.

This is an abuse of the past we claim to revere. The whole point of past blessings, past liturgies and Bible versions, is that they embodied an authentic encounter with God for their day. They were expressions of the wonder of meeting God in the *now*. Just as the best way to revere the Celtic saints is not to go misty eyed and dream of Ireland or Iona, but to learn to see our own world with the same clarity as they saw theirs, so the best way to honour renewal movements of the past is to encounter God afresh in our own day, in ways appropriate to the present.

Lots of otherwise intelligent Christian people have

73

their sights fixed on a dead past, convinced that in doing so they are honouring God. Meanwhile, the present ebbs away on a spiral of unwonder.

Past hurt or failure

Hurt and failure take many forms. They can be individual experiences – things I have done, or things that have been done to me – and they can also involve organizations, even whole nations.

A misjudgement which cost the company dear, a wrong career move, a relationship that ended badly, an own-goal which cost the team the championship. Some people keep returning to that moment, as if by replaying it they might be able to undo its effects. Convinced that it is to blame for their subsequent problems, they set their time-travel dial to this moment of failure.

Other dials are set to a moment when somebody else did something hurtful: the violence or harsh words of a parent, the experience of being bullied in school, the time a partner or close friend said something which implied rejection. This moment has acquired such devastating power that the only 'story' some people can now tell about their life is a story shaped by hurt.

As a child, Shona suffered at the hands of a violent father. He was a harsh, demanding man, always expecting more from his children than they could realistically offer. She carried deep inadequacy long into adult life. In her early 40s, hope appeared in the form of a group for victims of violent parents. At meetings, fellow members shared their own stories and offered mutual support. So far, so good. However, such was the friendship and support she gained from this group that Shona soon built her entire social life and identity around it.

Rather than helping Shona grow beyond her hurts, or releasing her to reach out to others like herself, the group has turned in on itself. It has become a time-travellers' group: people constantly returning to past pains, whose only identity is their victimhood. Rather than moving beyond the past, Shona keeps it alive by her regular trips in the time machine – only now, rather than going alone, she takes some friends and makes an outing of it. Perversely, parental abuse still dominates her life.

What is true of individuals can be true of families, organizations, even whole nations, each keeping alive a moment of past conflict: a family feud, a war, a schism. For many people the Reformation, the day your father insulted my brother, the Battle of the Boyne, the Crusades, the splitting of families in the American Civil War, are still all too vivid. Their memory has to be kept alive – lest we forget what the years of hatred have been about. Lest we forget the past.

But wonder is not located in the past. Nor is it located in the future.

Wonder postponed

Some of us are experts at postponing the moment when we stop and savour the wonder of life. At 15, we tell ourselves things will be fine once we have escaped from our crazy, repressive parents. At 25, we shall find the wonder of life once we have settled which line of work we prefer. At 35, life will be wonderful when babies have stopped screaming and we have unbroken nights of sleep. At 45, wonder will accompany that really big job promotion. At 55, we defer everything until retirement. Then we retire and realize most of life has gone.

I recently read a moving letter in my local newspaper. It was from an elderly woman who admitted she had never allowed herself to relax and enjoy life. Happiness was always in the future, postponed until after something else had happened first. Now in her 80s, she found she had spent a life free of wonder, joy and celebration. If she could have her time over again, she writes, she would take more risks, get less uptight, laugh more, be less focused on the destination and take more time to enjoy the journey.

Her time machine had always been set to a near future which never quite arrived. Her lifetime's indifference to the present moment had meant a lifetime lived on the spiral of unwonder.

Most time travellers have plausible excuses for postponing wonder: 'I don't have the time right now', 'I'm going through a difficult patch', 'I'll think about it when life's less complicated'. But these are more excuse than reality. Real life is rarely divided into stretches of busy/relaxed, difficult/easy, complex/simple. Every day has joys and wonders. Every day has troubles too. Don't postpone the wonder to the day when circumstances are more conducive to it. That day will never arrive.

Hypotheticals

Some people postpone the wonder of life to a near future. Others find wonder crushed beneath the weight of hypothetical futures, scenarios which never actually happen.

When Anna was a child, her house was filled with books of moving Christian testimonies: the man who learned wisdom through the tragic death of his wife, the girl who learned humility through a horrible accident, the church which grew through the pain of multiple bereavement. Partly through reading such books, Anna grew up expecting God to visit unbearable pain upon her and her family.

In her early 20s, she got engaged. But Anna could not savour the moment. She thought of the pain she would feel if her fiancé were to die early. In her imagination she watched him succumb to cancer, get mangled in a car crash, fall from upper-storey windows and be murdered by mad axemen. When her children were born, her joy was tempered by the sure knowledge that there had been a mix-up of children in the hospital, that her children would die horribly in a house fire or be abducted by perverts.

Hypothetical scenes have dominated Anna's life. The one thing she never allows herself to do is simply to relax, be grateful for what she has, and let tomorrow take care of itself. She seems to feel that forewarned is forearmed: if she has already played out the scenario in her imagination, she will not be caught off guard when it happens. The reality is that she has wasted time on unnecessary anguish. Mark Twain once remarked that he had been through some terrible things in his life – some of which actually happened!

This is not to downplay actual illness, bereavement and pain. At these times, the hurt we feel is all too real. But the point is this: the whole of life really can be experienced as something precious and wonder-filled, even a life full of suffering.

Paradoxically, many who live in the poorest countries, under the most adverse circumstances, often experience more wonder than those of us living in relatively affluent, trouble-free circumstances. I think of some of our neighbours, who arrived as refugees from the world's most horrific war-zones. Some escaped after seeing their family butchered and home destroyed. And still many of them manage to be positive, wonder-filled people. But maybe this is no paradox. Maybe they see the wonder of life because they know how fragile and precious a thing it is. They certainly make for an interesting contrast with some living in affluent suburbs, who descend into misery and anger at toothache, a mislaid hairbrush or a broken dishwasher.

Many of us are suffering a severe case of wondercidal hypotheticals. We have set the co-ordinates on our time machine so firmly to a hypothetical future that we never linger long enough in the present moment to savour that wonder.

Time on the spiral of unwonder

Wonder lies not in nostalgia for a glorious past, or reliving a painful past. It does not lie in postponing life indefinitely into the future, or being haunted by the spectre of an imagined future. As long as we set the co-ordinates on our time machine to one of these destinations, the only time zone we shall arrive at is the spiral of unwonder.

On that spiral, we invariably find ourselves indifferent to the present moment. We find now a boring place to be. We then allow ourselves to slip into fantasy: 'If only I hadn't done that as a child', 'If only I had passed that exam', 'If only I could be a student again', 'If only I were already retired', 'If only we hadn't had children', 'If only I could have had children', 'If only I hadn't been bullied as a child', 'If only my parents had brought me up differently', 'If only I could be 16 again'. If only, if only.

In consequence, we lose our ability to engage with the present moment and find wonder there. We withdraw. For the silent-screen actress Mary Pickford, withdrawal meant acute alcoholism. For others, it takes the form of drugs. For many more, it simply means a sad, aimless life, drained of colour: a life where either the hope of joy is futile, since the spring of wonder was dammed up long ago, or happiness is always just beyond the next mountain.

A sentence from the poet W. H. Auden expresses this feeling well. In his poetic Christmas drama, *For the Time Being*, he imagines the thoughts of the Wise Men as they pursued their journey to Bethlehem. His Second Wise Man expresses precisely this dilemma. For him, the wonder of life appears always to lie in the past or a receding future:

> With envy, terror, rage, regret,
> We anticipate or remember but never *are*.[2]

He goes on to say:

> To discover how to be living now
> Is the reason I follow this star.[3]

But what is the key to learning to live now? And what is the relevance of this quest for a star which hangs over an obscure Middle Eastern town? That is not only the quest of Auden's Wise Men. It is our quest too.

A short exercise

Just for a few moments, pause from reading this book. Put all thoughts and anxieties on hold for a while. Focus on your present circumstances.

Think about your own posture – whether you are sitting, lying or standing as you read. Think about where you are: the room, bus, train, garden. Maybe the sun is shining. Maybe you are in a comfortable chair. Maybe it is winter and there is frost in the air. Maybe you can hear distant sounds: birds singing, voices of children. Is there a fragrance in the room? Is it the fragrance of food, grass, new paint, exhaust fumes? Maybe this is your moment of peace after a busy day. Maybe you hear music playing.

Focus on this moment. Look at it. Listen to it. Touch it. Smell it. Savour it. Engage all your senses. Be grateful for it, because it will never come round again. Become aware of yourself doing the appreciating. You are alive. You have chosen to read this book. You have thoughts going through your head about what is written in it. You have a lot of things in your life to be grateful for. Now choose three special things from your current circumstances – even if they seem trivial – and be thankful for them.

* * * * *

Now start to think about your unfinished chores for the day. When will you fit them in? And your tasks for the coming week. When will you do those? Start to allow a little guilt in: have I been wasting my time reading this book, when I should have been doing something else? Will somebody be displeased with me? Now think about a difficult relationship you are currently in: at work, at home, or in the wider family. Recall the source of those difficulties.

Now think back to your most embarrassing moment. Relive how it made you feel. Think back to childhood. Was your upbringing as happy as that of some of your school friends? Couldn't your parents have done better? Tried harder? Now imagine how you might feel if the phone rang to say your closest friend had just fallen under a bus. Or if that faint mark on your arm turned out to be cancer.

See? Somewhere around that row of asterisks you slipped from the spiral of wonder to the spiral of unwonder. You stepped out of the present moment, and into your time machine, setting the co-ordinates for past or future, real or hypothetical.

But to experience time on the spiral of wonder is to be vibrantly alive to *now*. It is to encounter the present moment in a focused way, be grateful for it, and be passionately committed to it. To live in the now on the spiral of wonder is to travel by the scenic route and pause for picnics. It is to acknowledge where you have come from, and the destination to which you are travelling, but not to focus primarily on either of these. It is to enjoy the journey as something wonderful in itself.

The novelist Robert Louis Stevenson wrote that he loved to travel, simply for travel's sake. He enjoyed simply going on a journey.[4] If we learn to apply Stevenson's principle to our experience of the passing of time – loving each moment, for its own sake – we shall find the wonder of life begins to return. We shall no longer be constantly wishing away the present moment. I live now for what now has to offer, not because it is an appendix to the past, or a road to a brighter future. Now, in itself, can be a moment of wonder.

Once again, we can find sharp insights and helpful guidelines in a place most people never think to look: the Bible. There, we find both a model for living in the present moment, and also guidelines on the means of achieving this ourselves. The model is found in the life of Jesus Christ. The means are set out in the letters of the apostle Paul.

ENCOUNTER, GRATITUDE, COMMITMENT

Living for today

One of the great mysteries of the ages is the process by which the Jesus of the Gospels became insipid in the popular imagination. When, in 1866 the Victorian poet Algernon Swinburne wrote scathingly of Jesus, 'Thou hast conquered, O pale Galilean; the world has grown grey from thy breath',[5] he was reflecting a common view of Jesus that has survived to the present day. It is the image of a pallid, dull teacher of morals, who frowned on living for the present moment and pointed rather to a vague afterlife, way beyond the blue. Such an image has been reinforced by portraits of Jesus in sentimental Western art.

However, the briefest blast of Middle Eastern heat from the Gospels quickly dispels the pallor. The biblical Jesus, unlike Swinburne's, is a robust and passionate young man – confrontational, charismatic, emotional, apocalyptic, urgent in his call that we should seize the present moment. In Mark's Gospel the first recorded words of Jesus are a summons to an immediate response: 'The time has come', he said. 'The kingdom of God is near. Repent and believe the good news' (Mark 1.15).

For Jesus, the new life offered by God begins not after death, but now: 'I tell you the truth, whoever hears my word and believes him who sent me *has* eternal life' (John 5.24, my emphasis).

His challenge to a tax collector called Levi is brisk and immediate – 'Follow me' (Mark 2.14) – and he is scathing about those who delay commitment (such as the man who first wants to bury his dead father, Luke 9.59–60). He teaches his followers to pray, 'Give us today our daily bread' (Matthew 6.11), just as he teaches them to pray for the breaking in of God's rule to the present day, and tells them that their moral 'debts' from the past will be forgiven (the idea of sin as a 'debt' owed to God was common at the time), as they forgive other people, freeing them to live fully in the present.

The breathless style of Mark's Gospel in particular reinforces the immediacy of the message. Mark's Greek words, *kai euthus* ('at once' or 'straight away'), appear 11 times in the opening chapter alone, and 40 times in the whole Gospel. Frequently, Mark uses the historic present tense in narrating the events. In Mark 1.12, for example, the Greek actually reads, 'the Spirit drives him out into the wilderness'. This gives a sense of immediacy, by telling a past event as if it were happening now. New Testament scholar Richard Burridge says of Mark's use of the historic present:

> Occasionally this can help bring any story suddenly alive, but Mark does it 151 times in his gospel, which perhaps is a trifle excessive! This is why many English versions do not translate these as present tenses, remaining in past time. Unfortunately this means that we miss Mark's vividness and pace.[6]

Not only does Jesus live in the present moment, and call others to do the same, he denies that there is safety in looking back to the past or dreaming of a vague future. Jesus condemns those who wistfully look back to the past: 'Still another said, "I will follow you, Lord; but first let me go back and say good-bye to my family." Jesus replied, "No one who puts his hand to the plough and looks back is fit for service in the kingdom of God"' (Luke 9.62). But to those weighed down by an onerous past he offers present respite: 'Come to me all you who are weary and burdened, and I will give you rest' (Matthew 11.28).

He attacks the 'rich fool' who thinks he can plan for the future by storing up grain in ever bigger barns (Luke 12.16–21), and those who are constantly anxious about the basics of life, such as food and clothing (Luke 12.22–34). Indeed, in Matthew's version of this teaching, Jesus is quite explicit: 'Therefore do not worry about tomorrow, for tomorrow will worry about itself. Each day has enough trouble of its own' (Matthew 6.34).

No, says Jesus, we are not to live in regret for the triumphs and failures of the past. Nor are we to live in the future, either in fantasy or anxiety. Rather, we are to live life recklessly, passionately and to the full, which means a quality of life only he can bring: 'I have come that they may have life, and have it to the full' (John 10.10). And this fullness of life begins here and now: 'Whoever hears my word and believes him who sent me has eternal life and will not be condemned; he has crossed over from death to life' (John 5.24).

This is an offer which can't be ignored by anybody concerned about rediscovering wonder. Jesus Christ offers nothing less than a life lived on the spiral of wonder: life, now, in all its joyful wildness.

Freed to find wonder in the now

If the reckless fullness of life seen in the person and teaching of Jesus is our destination, Paul is our guide. His letters to first-century Christian churches still offer valuable insights into the quest for wonder restored. Paul offers concrete and specific rebuttals of every attempt to view time from the spiral of unwonder. He points the way to freedom from our time-travelling dead-ends: nostalgia, past failure, past hurts, postponing wonder and hypothetical scenarios. We shall look briefly at each.

Freed from nostalgia

According to Paul, the Christian gospel frees us from nostalgia for a golden past, for one simple reason. Past glories count for nothing. In the book of Acts (22.1–5) and his letter to the Philippians (3.4–6), Paul tells how he has more reason than any to boast of his past: he was of the finest pedigree, studied under the finest teacher of the day, quickly climbed the career ladder, was zealous in faith and scrupulous in his adherence to religious law.

But Paul's conversion, in his early 30s, changed all that. Something so energized the present that the glories of his past became as nothing:

> But whatever was to my profit I now consider loss for the sake of Christ. What is more, I consider everything a loss compared to the surpassing greatness of knowing Christ Jesus my Lord, for whose sake I have lost all things. I consider them rubbish, that I may gain Christ. (Philippians 3.7–8)

His encounter with the risen Christ now made every day a journey of adventure and wonder. Paul was not a killjoy, abandoning past achievements out of a perverse masochism. He was a man living on the spiral of wonder, whose present had become so filled with wonder that even the best moments of the past paled into insignificance.

If the apostle Paul saw even his exalted past as 'rubbish', our nostalgia too begins to look suspiciously like rooting through an old case of mothballed junk.

Freed from past failure

We can not only be freed from nostalgia, says Paul; we can also be freed from past failure. The word Paul uses for this is 'grace'. Grace remains one of the most frequently used words in the Christian vocabulary – and one of the least understood. But a rediscovery of Paul's wonder at God's grace has been behind practically every significant renewal movement in church history.

Human instinct tends towards seeing God as a judge. Most people appear to assume that God sits, aloof from his world, with a pair of old-fashioned scales. Into one pan he places our good deeds, into the other he puts the things we do wrong. At the end of the day, if our good deeds outweigh the bad, we are in.

Some religious people prefer an image of chalk and slate, because it adds a note of repentance and forgiveness. In this picture, God sits with an old-fashioned slate or blackboard. Whenever we sin, he chalks a mark on it. If we remain stubbornly unrepentant, the marks remain and count against us. But if we repent, God wipes it clean – at least for the time being – and we are forgiven. According to this image, life is a gradual build-up of chalk marks, and a periodic erasing of them after repentance.

Both pictures make sense. They seem logical. But neither the scales nor the slate is Christianity. In fact, for all their popularity, both images represent a denial of the gospel. What does Paul say instead? 'But because of his great love for us, God, who is rich in mercy, *made us alive with Christ even while we were dead in transgressions* – it is by *grace* you have been saved' (Ephesians 2.4–5, my emphasis).

Grace means God offering people a wonder-filled encounter with himself, absolutely without precondition. Grace is God's limitless love and full acceptance of people who don't deserve it. It means that God throws away the scales, slate and stock of chalk. This has extraordinary consequences.

It means that for those who are 'in Christ' (open to receiving this grace, committed to Christ), the sins and failings of the past are binned, as God forgives them. It also means that even the sins and failings we haven't committed yet are already thrown away. We are guaranteed forgiveness in advance.

If that sounds outrageous, unjust, too good to be true, or open to abuse, then we have started to grasp the heart of the gospel. The Christian offer of salvation really is scandalous and risky, and isn't dependent on our being good or deserving enough, or learning correct spiritual techniques. In fact, the New Testament hints that it is the good and religious who are least likely to understand and accept grace.

Grace means that from God's perspective, the wrongs we do – or the wrongs we might do in future – can never be an obstacle to our finding the wonder of relationship with him. Our sins and virtues are not the issue. The only possible obstacle is our own refusal to accept God's free gift of grace. Of course, once we have been bowled over by a grace that comes without precondition, we desire – like Paul – to live a life pleasing to God. But that is a separate issue. The grace which erases the past and embraces God is downloaded totally free of charge.

Grace frees us to encounter the present moment. Guilt and shame from past failures hold us back. They condemn us to a life in the time machine, travelling backwards on the spiral of unwonder. Without grace, as we look out from our time machine and contemplate the future, we see only a grim cycle of repeated failure: never knowing if we can become good enough, or if we have prayed for forgiveness enough. Our awareness of past failure and the inevitability of future failure can only paralyse the present.

Grace, the good news that God has left the weighing and counting business, bins the whole sorry process of sin, guilt and backward time travel. The theme is so central to Paul's own experience, and his way of making sense of life, that he returns to it dozens of times (for example, Romans 3.24; 1 Corinthians 15.10; Colossians 1.6). God's grace, says Paul, is our freedom to be. It is God's 'No' to our being bound by past failure, his 'Yes' to our living life in all its fullness, here and now.

Freed from past hurts

Jenny rushes excitedly to Tania's office. 'I've got it!' she cries. 'Got what?' asks Tania. 'The answer for what to do about Pete, of course,' says Jenny.

'OK. So what are you going to do about Pete?'

'Listen. You know how he always walks past me when I'm standing by the photocopier, and pats my backside? I tell you, it's the last time he ever does that. Pete thinks because he's my boss, he can get away with anything. Well, he can't. Tomorrow I'll be ready for him. I'm going to hang a small packet of explosives from my belt – and then when he pats me on the backside, BOOM! – he blows his hand off!'

I admit it. This is a ludicrous illustration. Nobody would ever do something like that. We all know that in such a case, we would only be getting even with our enemy by damaging our own body. But this is no more ludicrous than something many of us do routinely, something commonplace and unremarkable: our failure to forgive.

John and Sally have been married 15 years. In the early days Sally felt daunted by the level of commitment demanded by the new relationship. Her own parents' marriage, and those of other relatives, had seemed to her routine and dutiful, rather than fun and life-enhancing. She was nervous that her own marriage might descend to this level too. One day the couple were walking in the woods, arguing. During the course of the argument, in anger, Sally found herself saying she wished she had never married John. He was devastated. The words burned deep into his mind.

Years passed. Sally's anxieties about the marriage subsided. As she relaxed, she threw herself more and more into the marriage. But John never forgot the words spoken in the wood. Never mind that the marriage itself was clearly working well. Never mind that there had been mitigating circumstances: Sally's anxieties early on, the fact that she had been going through a bad patch at work, the fact that at the time John had been preoccupied with work and less openly affectionate than usual.

All that mattered to John was what she'd said. She must have meant it. After all, if she hadn't meant it, why would she have said something so devastating? He regularly called to mind those words, especially during arguments. He took them as her considered opinion on him and the marriage. To him, the marriage might have fun moments, but he could never be fully committed to it. He always held something back. How can a man be wholly committed to a wife who wishes she had never married him?

Ten years into the marriage it struck John that he had to forgive Sally. He had to make a conscious decision to let go of the words in the wood, to stop feeding his resentment. The victim of his unforgiveness was his own marriage – and, ultimately, his own happiness. He found that for years he had been getting back at his tormentor by damaging himself. When he forgave, a great burden was lifted from himself. The past became the past, and he was freed to enjoy the present and make a good marriage better.

Grace is God's forgiveness of us, even when we do not deserve it. Forgiveness is our response to this grace, when we stretch it to encompass all our relationships. It is allowing the past to be the past, freeing ourselves and others from its tyranny, surrendering our right to get even, making ours the first step towards reconciliation and healing. Even if the other person remains unrepentant. Even if they do not want our forgiveness.

Paul understood the power of forgiveness. He had been forgiven much, and now found he had to forgive others in the same measure. His advice to Christians in the Turkish city of Colossae is timeless in its relevance: 'Bear with each other and forgive whatever grievances you may have against one another. Forgive as the Lord forgave you' (Colossians 3.13).

We have looked at nostalgia, failure and hurts: three instances where the past can become a prison, a place where we may be held captive. Does the past, then, have no place in the life of wonder? This point needs to be clarified.

To live on the spiral of wonder is not to dismiss the past. Rather, it is a way of living which has learned an appropriate relationship to the past: as something that resources the present. This resourcing includes identity-formation (I am who I am because of my own unique history). It also includes learning (my freedom and ability to speak French or play the guitar today are only made possible by hours of study in the past). And for the Christian, the past is supremely a place of revelation: it reveals God's dealings with humanity through history. Christians find their own identity and calling only in the context of God's past actions. They read the Bible as the record of God's self-revealing – and they do this not as an escape from today, but as a rich resource for it.

So the past is vital and life-giving when it equips, empowers and releases us. But all too often we allow it to become our jailer.

Freed from postponing wonder

Some are prevented from finding the wonder of the present by being locked in the past. And we saw that some never find the wonder of life and faith because they are always postponing it to another day. To such people Paul has a blunt challenge: 'I tell you, *now* is the time of God's favour, *now* is the day of salvation (2 Corinthians 6.2, my emphasis). Paul's letters, like the ministry of Jesus, itch with a sense of urgency: 'The time is short' (1 Corinthians 7.29). Get on with it, says Paul. Fullness of life begins now.

But isn't Paul also preoccupied by the future return of Christ, and eternity in the presence of God? Isn't this the same man who talks about the life of faith as a race, with the athlete's eyes set on the prize that awaits him (1 Corinthians 9.24; Philippians 3.14)? How, then, can we say that Paul finds wonder in the present when he is so firmly focused on the future?

As with the past, there are right lenses and wrong lenses through which we can view the future. The wrong lens is that of fantasy. Seen through this lens, the future is an escape from the present. We jump into our time machine and imagine that one day, things will somehow improve: when we have left home, met a partner, retired, and so on. But the fantasy never quite becomes a reality. Wonder is always deferred to another day.

Paul is no fantasizer. The lens through which he views the future is that of hope. Paul writes that God's grace not only frees us from the past, and frees us to embrace fullness of life in the present, it also frees us to have a right view of the future. In a short letter to Titus, one of his Gentile converts, he writes: 'God . . . saved us . . . so that having been justified by his grace, we might become heirs of the *hope* of eternal life' (Titus 3.4–7, my emphasis).

Fantasy is a flight from the present, whereas hope resources it. Paul has a clear vision of the future: a glorious return of Christ, the transformation of our bodies into resurrection bodies like Christ's (Philippians 3.21), an eternity with Christ. Because he has a solid hope, the present is filled with meaning: it gives him an urgent task to be getting on with. But even here, the present does not just mean working for a future blessing. Like Jesus, Paul emphasizes that for the believer, the wonder of eternity has already begun. The future hope is not something separate from the present, but an extension of it. C. S. Lewis writes on the biblical understanding of hope:

A continual looking forward to the eternal world is not (as some modern people think) a form of escapism or wishful thinking . . . It does not mean that we are to leave the present world as it is. If you read history you will find that the Christians who did most for the present world were just those who thought most of the next . . . It is since Christians have largely ceased to think of the other world that they have become so ineffective in this. Aim at Heaven and you will get earth 'thrown in': aim at earth and you will get neither.[7]

It is the difference between a young girl who fantasizes that one day her prince will come, and the girl who knows her fiancé is coming round that evening. The one sits and reads escapist novels, and her thoughts are so far away that she neglects to do the dishes or tidy her flat. Her mind is fixed on far pavilions and enchanted castles. But the other rushes around getting herself and her flat ready for the arrival. She wants to be at her best when her very real lover stands at the door.

Fantasy and hope are opposite lenses for viewing the future. The one views the present with resignation and apathy, the other with excitement and wonder. The one encourages passivity, the other action. The one drains the present of meaning, the other fills it with meaning. The one is a place on the spiral of unwonder, the other on the spiral of wonder.

The Talmud, the collection of rabbis' teaching on the Hebrew Scriptures, says that everybody, some time in their life, should have a child, plant a tree and write a book. This is hope of a very earthy variety. Each of these activities is orientated to the future: a child will become part of the next generation of adults; a tree will grow for years to come; a book preserves thoughts and feelings for future readers. But each also gives meaning and wonder to the present moment: sex, gardening and creativity.

Freed from hypotheticals

Finally, Paul offers a key to freedom from hypotheticals, those anxious scenarios which many of us play out in our minds, but which rarely happen. Such hypotheticals are time's equivalent of the rampant 'If Onlys' which gnaw away at our wonder: What if she dies early? What if that lump turns out to be cancer? What if they don't return home at the time they said? What if . . . ?

Paul's remedy for a severe case of the hypotheticals is to focus on giving thanks: 'Be joyful always; pray continually; give thanks in all circumstances, for this is God's will for you in Christ Jesus' (1 Thessalonians 5.16–18). To give thanks is to focus on the present. It is to enjoy what we have, and become more committed to it. It is to count our blessings, not our nightmares.

Paul on the spiral of wonder

In Chapter Two we looked at Paul as an example of a man alive on the spiral of wonder. Here we have seen his insights on finding wonder. It means being freed from nostalgia, failure and past hurts. It means freedom from our tendency to postpone wonder and drift into fantasy. It involves encounter with the present moment, thanks for it, and commitment to living in it. The keys to achieving this include receiving grace, offering forgiveness and cultivating gratitude.

And at the heart of it all stands one figure, compelling and inescapable: that of Jesus of Nazareth.

CHAPTER FIVE

AT THE HEART
OF WONDER

Wonder is the basis of worship.

(Thomas Carlyle)

'A-grade' wonder

Let's summarize some points already made. For the apostle Paul, 'A-grade' wonder is only accessible through theism – faith in a supreme, personal God. Only theism tells us why we feel the gratitude so essential to wonder. We feel grateful because everything we have, everything around us, is a gift – and that gift has a giver. More specifically, says Paul, 'A-grade' wonder centres on the figure of Jesus Christ. Only in Christ can we access the grace that is a vital precondition for fullness of life. And only in Christ are we empowered to forgive, and move beyond nostalgia and fantasy.

Paul's meaning is clear. At the heart of wonder is a person: Jesus Christ. So we cannot consider the word 'wonder' without launching into an exploration of related ideas, such as faith, spirituality and worship.

This raises an obvious problem. If wonder is linked to spirituality, how is it that so many religious people are wonder-free zones? How can a spiritual descendent of Paul, whose every fibre tingled with urgency, gratitude and passion, live a life which is bland, complacent and passionless? When I was a teenager a schoolfriend, Jo, put it this way: 'If Christianity promises so much, and is supposed to be so wonderful, how come I find it so dull, and all the churches I go to are so boring?' This chapter is for people like Jo, for whom the promises of faith and its reality still seem poles apart.

Tragically, even the life of faith can be lived in unwonder. So negative are some people's experiences of church that they assume (wrongly but not unreasonably) that faith always equals unwonder. They then give up on church in disgust. The spiral of religious unwonder passes through familiar places: indifference, fantasy and withdrawal.

INDIFFERENCE AND WITHDRAWAL

In many parts of the world, the Christian Church is exploding with growth and excitement. In many parts of North America and Europe, too, church life has never been more creative or so passionate. But the over-all picture in these two continents is one of steady decline, particularly in mainline denominations. Around 53,000 churchgoers leave churches in Europe and North America every single week, and new recruitment – while exciting and often dramatic – is not keeping pace.[1] Reasons for the exodus include:

- A decline in the duty-churchgoing of an earlier era.
- A rise in alternative Sunday leisure activities: shopping, sport, car boot sales.
- Services which are uninspiring and irrelevant to everyday life.
- Graceless religion which focuses on morality and judgement.
- Religion without awe, reduced to easy soundbites.
- Religion without passion, reduced to empty ritual.

- Burnout: some simply cannot take the endless services, meetings and church activities.

Some people withdraw bitter and disillusioned, some
angry, others merely yawning. But the scale of the
exodus from the churches in Europe and North America
highlights one clear and alarming fact: millions of
people – millions of churchgoers – have been missing
God in church. Somewhere along the line, the wonder
of faith found by the likes of Paul has become boring,
judgemental or simply irrelevant.

FANTASY

Plenty do stay. But of those who do, many are victims
of fantasy faith. Fantasy faith works more subtly than
simple indifference and withdrawal. People put up
with it for longer before disillusionment sets in. But in
the long run, it proves just as corrosive of true wonder.
Fantasy faith is just another place on the spiral of
unwonder.

What is fantasy faith? It is a faith whose preachers,
teachers and gurus are the wild 'If Onlys' roaming
our imaginations, an escapist faith which believes that
wonder always lies somewhere else. It comes in a number of forms – we shall look at five of them in turn.

Waiting for the big event

Many worshippers put the wonder and joy of faith on
hold until some great, future event has happened.
Sometimes this event is a revival.

Revivals happen, and when they do the results can
be dramatic. During periods such as the Great
Awakening in eighteenth-century America, the Welsh
revival of 1904–5, the Korean revivals of the first decade
of the twentieth century, and the East African revival

96

of the 1930s, astonishing things happened. People came to faith in their thousands. Men and women walking down the street would suddenly become overwhelmed with a need of God, and would be converted on the spot. The words of a witness of the Hebridean revival of 1949 are typical: 'It seemed as if the very air was electrified with the Spirit of God...There was an awesomeness of the presence of God.'[2]

But there is a fine line between praying for revival, and the escapism which puts everything on hold until revival is here. Many Christians talk in excitement of 'when revival comes', and 'when God moves in power'. Hope and expectation are fine things. But postponing the wonder and passion of faith to an unspecified date in the future is risky, for at least two reasons.

One is that God might not send revival – at least, not in a form we expect or recognize. For all our prayer, preaching and fervour, revival is ultimately a sovereign act of God. And most Christians, at most points in history, have not been living during 'revival'. We need to accept that the fireworks we long for might not come. This is hard to accept for people in a consumer culture, who can usually get anything they want if they want it enough.

Without the fireworks, what of the wonder of faith? For many it ends up as dashed as their hopes. Many feel resentful and misled. To be real, Christian faith has to be rooted in the person of Christ, not an event which might or might not happen.

The other problem is that revival is merely icing on a cake. Even if it does come, it will not replace a balanced diet of prayer, study, service and worship. It presupposes that believers are already getting on with the business of everyday spirituality. Revival travels along a road already made smooth by the hard reality of a daily, ongoing pilgrimage.

Some postpone 'getting down to business with God' until some other big event has happened: for Jack it was the hope of entering the ministry. But Jack was still struggling with some major personal issues when he came to discuss the matter with me. His faith was shaky at crucial points. His own sense of self-worth was perilously low. And he was plagued by unresolved lifestyle questions.

Not that aspiring ministers have to be perfect. But Jack still had a distance to go before ordination could become an appropriate course. Otherwise, his personal demons might cause havoc not only to himself but also to others. Jack believed ordination would magically solve his personal problems, that he could carry on limping along in faith and lifestyle until ordination put everything to rights. I had to point out that, sadly, it didn't work that way.

We all have our excuses: when I've had that big experience which removes my doubts, when the new church is built, when the new minister comes, when I go on retreat, when we start that new community project, when I join a religious community. Forget it. This is the language not of hope, but a voracious 'If Only'. Encounter with Christ happens here and now. Big event or no big event.

Waiting for the big experience

Some wait for a big spiritual experience to kick-start their faith. This might mean waiting to be 'zapped' by the power of God and falling over, or being so overwhelmed by the Spirit that they double up as if in pain, or burst into helpless laughter.

In a different church tradition it might be waiting for a numinous experience which lifts the soul heavenward, triggered by the perfection of the architecture, the poetry of the words, the purity of the music. For contemplatives and mystics, it might be reaching a stage in the contemplative life: a moment when they feel themselves absorbed into God, transcending the body, achieving a state of inner tranquillity, or a 'higher' or 'deeper' level of spirituality.

It is true that the Christian life can involve a range of experiences, some powerful and moving. But many believers spend their entire lives feeling spiritually second-rate, waiting for a big experience that will raise them from the merely humdrum to the super-saint. But this is spiritual fantasy-land.

Much of what we crave has less to do with spirituality than personality. Some of us will never experience being 'zapped' in dramatic fashion at a revival meeting. There is no great mystery as to why. We encounter God. But when we do, the channel God uses includes the temperament he equipped us with and the expectations shaped by our church tradition.

When someone in the pew next to you sobs uncontrollably during sermons, speaks as if they have a hotline to God, and falls over at the end of every service, it is tempting to feel inadequate. Don't. What you are seeing is not sheer, unmediated God-power. It is what happens when a particular type of person encounters God. You are seeing God-power as filtered through a particular person's temperament and the expectations they have learned from a certain type of church. The same encounter may provoke in you a feeling of inner calm, or a desire to study theology. That person is just different from you.

Or maybe you are surrounded by people whose encounter with God makes them go dreamy and silent, adopting the long-suffering look of a medieval saint. By contrast with them, you feel clumsy, loud and unspiritual. Again, don't feel that way. What you are seeing is simply what happens when a different sort of person, with a different set of expectations, meets God.

The worst option of all is to assume that the ecstasies the next person is experiencing are the form that all fervent faith ought to take – and then to fake it. We each encounter God in different ways. Relax and enjoy the diversity.

Another reason many of us look at our Christian lives and see something mundane is that we are unrealistic in our expectations. We idealize life in New Testament times as if faith and holiness were easy, revival constant and miracles abounded. However, this fantasy founders on two hard realities. One is that for most of the biblical period – Old and New Testament alike – most people never met God, heard a heavenly voice, met an angel or saw a miracle. The glory moments were the exception rather than the rule. Most believers in biblical times were called, like us, to a journey which was mostly trust and endurance, with no burning bush or floating axe-head to silence nagging doubts. One of the towering figures of the Old Testament, David, never experienced a single 'miracle' of the type some well-meaning preachers today tell us to expect daily.[3]

The second hard reality to accept, for those of us who view Bible times with a golden glow of nostalgia, is that being in the thick of the glory usually made no long-term difference to those who experienced it. They fell away, grumbled, apostasized, rebelled and doubted just as we do.[4] Solomon, for example, had two breathtaking encounters with God. And he still ended up on the spiral of unwonder: adrift in cynicism, and sexual and spiritual promiscuity.

I must emphasize that I believe God performs signs and wonders – and the Christian life can include moments of sheer ecstasy. But we have no right to expect these moments to be anything other than outstanding exceptions. It is a cheapened, consumerized spirituality that demands an ever stronger 'fix', a spirituality for a drug culture.

Our fantasies of big spiritual experiences, 'higher' and 'deeper' states, and our coveting of other people's apparently more ecstatic moments, can be hindrances to the process of real spirituality, which is earthy, everyday and unpretentious. Encounter with Christ begins here and now, in the mundane details of everyday life, or not at all.

Waiting for the right technique

It was 1994. The minister had returned from Canada, seeing first-hand the excitement of the 'Toronto blessing'. I attended one of the meetings he held on his return to London. That evening he recreated gesture-by-gesture, word-for-word what he had seen in Toronto. When things appeared to be flagging, he shouted, 'More, Lord! More, Lord!' over and over, just as they had done in Toronto. Every word, every angle of the arm, every shake and laugh, was a Toronto clone. The whole evening was a painstaking attempt to recreate the Toronto experience.

For all his faith and sincerity, this minister was falling for the fantasy of correct technique: 'If only I do things right, the right results will occur, just as they did last time.' Rather than looking to God to do a fresh and distinct thing in his own parish, he could only envisage a Toronto franchise.

This bears an uncomfortable resemblance to magic – not conjuring tricks, but the type of magic widely practised in the ancient world and by occultists today. Such magic is essentially an attempt to harness spiritual forces to do the will of the magician. And the key to achieving this is the use of the right incantation, spell, password and gestures. In a word, magic is all about getting technique right.

At the other end of the ecclesiastical spectrum from the Toronto minister, an Anglo-Catholic friend insists there is only one valid type of priest, one way to celebrate Holy Communion, with one set of priestly 'manual acts', one appropriate style of church music, and that the Spirit is only dispensed through the hands of a particular sort of bishop. As we shall see, our diverse church traditions have a valuable place in the life of faith and search for wonder. But when any worship tradition becomes rigid and absolutist, when it elevates correct technique beyond its proper place, as one aid among many towards the goal of encountering Christ, it degenerates into something approaching magic.

God is not a genie of the lamp, summoned up by the person who has secret knowledge, or knows special words or actions. God is sovereign and personal. The Spirit blows where he will. Worship is like sex: once we lose the wonder of personal encounter, all that remains is technique.

When I'm good enough

Here is an excuse used by many on the fringes of the Church for delaying commitment. They picture the Church as a club for the morally upright, and they know they are just not like that. One day, they reason, they might settle down and become a nicer, kinder person. Then they might reconsider faith. In its more overtly Christian form, this involves postponing full commitment 'until I have sorted out this one sin', 'until I'm further down the road of being holy'.

Either way, it is sheer fantasy. Grace means that God accepts us for who we are, even before we have begun to think about improvement. To postpone the wonder of faith until we are good enough is to postpone it for ever. Encounter with Christ begins here and now, with all our failings and immoralities, or not at all.

Thomas Cook spirituality

Some people's spiritual fantasy is that their spiritual life will be put to rights if they journey to some place of pilgrimage. This might be Toronto, Geneva, Pensacola, Walsingham, Rome, Jerusalem, Lourdes, Spring Harvest, Keswick, Taizé, Istanbul, Los Angeles or Wheaton.

Pilgrimage can be a moving experience. To travel to a site which has rich historical associations, and is close to the roots of our faith, can be inspiring. But to defer encounter with Christ until we tread a particular piece of holy ground is to abuse pilgrimage. We travel to gain fresh inspiration for a wonder-filled encounter with home, not because the wonder lies elsewhere.

The real task is, as we have seen, to become pilgrims in our own parish: people who realize, like Moses, that the very earth we walk upon is holy ground. Here is the place we encounter Christ. Here and now.

FACE TO FACE WITH JESUS

To experience the glory of faith on the spiral of wonder is to encounter Jesus Christ, and to be filled with gratitude for who he is and what he has done. But what does it mean to encounter Christ? To begin finding out, we need to put ourselves in the place of those who met him face to face.

Meeting Jesus

In the Gospels, those who meet Jesus react to the experience in remarkably similar ways. They are overcome by a sense of wonder. The verb *thaumazo* keeps appearing in the original Greek to describe people's responses to Jesus. It means 'to be filled with wonder', or 'to be amazed'. As we study people's reactions more closely, we find that this word carries a range of emotions: being surprised or astonished, as by a miracle; being attracted and drawn to Jesus, as to one you love; and being filled with fear, awe – even terror – as in the presence of a great king or something beyond your understanding.

Where, then, do we find these encounters filled with the surprise, attraction and fear which make up *thaumazo*? In the crowds by the Sea of Galilee who heard Jesus' teaching (Matthew 15.31), at his healing of a demoniac (Matthew 9.33), in his teaching in the synagogue at Nazareth (Luke 4.22), in the astonishment of the disciples who witness him stilling a storm (Luke 8.25), during his trial before the Roman governor Pontius Pilate (Mark 15.5), at his death on the cross (Mark 15.44), in his resurrection appearances to his disciples (Luke 24.41).

The conception and birth of Jesus were greeted with wonder right from the start: Mary's combination of wonder and fear in the presence of Gabriel (Luke 1.26–38), the shepherds' telling of the nativity story (Luke 2.18), and Mary and Joseph's response to the words spoken over their child by the elderly Simeon in the Temple at Jerusalem (Luke 2.33). At the coming of Jesus, everyday prose becomes insufficient to convey the sense of wonder evoked in people's hearts. They break spontaneously into song and poetry: Mary (Luke 1.46–55), Zechariah (Luke 1.67–79), the angels (Luke 2.14), and Simeon (Luke 2.29–32).

After the resurrection and ascension of Jesus, the Jerusalem crowd on the day of Pentecost responds with wonder to the coming of the Spirit of Jesus (Acts 2.7), as do the witnesses of Peter and John's healing of a blind beggar in the name of Jesus (Acts 3.12).

A clear pattern emerges. To encounter the man Jesus, the risen Jesus, and the Spirit of Jesus, is to be filled with wonder: a wonder which combines joyful surprise, ecstatic love and attraction, but also a fear at finding yourself in the presence of something majestic and holy, untamed and unpredictable.

But aren't we at a massive disadvantage, compared to the New Testament witnesses? Can this kind of encounter still be found today? Actually, it can. In a word, we find it as we worship.

ENCOUNTER

The English word 'worship' comes from an Anglo-Saxon root, *worth-ship*, to ascribe worth and honour to some-body. In the Book of Common Prayer wedding service, the bridegroom tells his bride, 'With my body I thee worship'. He is telling her that she alone is worthy of his undying devotion. It is a statement of commitment and awe. Worship is about encounter, love and praise.

Some churches have truncated worship to mean a time of singing. But worship is richer and more holistic than that. A fuller vision of worship includes several ideas, each centred on a very real encounter with Christ: lifestyle, public worship, personal prayer, Bible study and receiving the sacraments of Holy Communion and baptism.

Lifestyle

We must begin with lifestyle because, although the most important, this is most easily overlooked. Worship is not limited to church services. These make up a fraction of our worship. Paul, writing to Rome, defines worship not primarily as words spoken or sung to God, but as the offering of a whole life and lifestyle to God, so we live in a way that challenges the values of our culture: 'Offer your bodies as living sacrifices, holy and pleasing to God – *this is your spiritual act of worship*. Do not conform any longer to the pattern of this world, but be transformed by the renewing of your mind (Romans 12.1–2, my emphasis).

Paul exhorts his readers in Colossae to see all they do as an act of worship to God: work (Colossians 3.23–4), sexuality (3.5–7), speech (3.8–10) and family life (3.18–21). He tells them that everything they do, as believers, 'whether in word or deed, do it all in the name of the Lord Jesus' (3.17).

Jesus himself tells us that the heart of worship is a lifestyle of hospitality and service. In his hard-hitting parable of the sheep and goats (Matthew 25.31–46), Jesus tells his followers that they are to develop a lifestyle which cares for those whom society marginalizes. Not only that, but every act of service we do for people who are needy, imprisoned and sick is actually done for him. This is a staggering claim. We personally encounter Christ in the dregs of society. He is there, if only we will look closely.

The fourth-century French saint, Martin of Tours, experienced this for himself. As a young soldier in the Roman army he was stationed near the town of Amiens. One cold day he was patrolling the city with a group of other soldiers, each wrapped in the heavy cloaks which were standard military issue. By the city gates they met a beggar who was close to freezing. To the ridicule of his colleagues, Martin drew his sword and cut his cloak in two, giving half to the beggar. That evening Martin had a vision of heaven, in which Christ himself was wearing the same cloak he had given away earlier. In the vision, Christ says, 'See! This is the cloak Martin gave me today.'

Jesus and Paul are not introducing a new idea when they equate lifestyle and worship. It is there in the words that God spoke to Israel through the Old Testament prophets. There, God defines the sort of worship he wants. He tells the people that formal religious worship comes a poor second to a lifestyle of justice and compassion – and that without such a lifestyle, worship in word and song is meaningless (see Isaiah 58.6–14, Amos 5.21–4, Hosea 6.6, etc.).

Again the message is reinforced: lifestyle is not incidental to worship. It is at the heart of it. As we show care and hospitality to those thrown away by society, those who make most people feel uneasy, that is where we may encounter Christ.

Public worship

If our primary worship is lifestyle, then why bother with public worship at all? This is not a facetious question. It springs naturally from the biblical insight that the main place we worship is our everyday life and lifestyle. If our understanding of public worship is as a retreat from the real world, a 'sacred' space as opposed to the 'secular' space of normal life, then public worship may well be an obstacle. We should be better off without a 'worship' which disables the real business of living for Christ in the world.

But in the same letter in which Paul tells his readers that their lifestyle is their worship, he also encourages them to meet to 'sing psalms, hymns and spiritual songs with gratitude in your hearts to God' (Colossians 3.16). Clearly, public worship has a place. This is for three main reasons: public worship is a reminder that we belong to a wider body of Christians, it is the training centre which equips us to find the wonder of everyday life, and it is quality time with Christ. All three involve encounter.

First, public worship is meeting with other believers. Paul's most potent image to describe the Church is the 'body of Christ'. For Paul, a solitary Christian is a contradiction in terms. His body metaphor reveals both our dependence on other believers (each limb can only reach its potential as part of the body, not by going it alone), and our unity with Christ (he is the 'head' of the body, of which we are part). Corporate worship is not just membership of a club. It is a visible expression of believers' organic unity, outside which we have no claim to be Christians, and through which Christ is at work in his world. Believe it or not, we encounter something of Christ in each other as we worship together.

Finding our place in the body, rather than by being spiritual loners, has the added benefit of encouraging us in our faith. St John of the Cross, a sixteenth-century Spanish mystic, said: 'The soul that is alone is like the burning coal that is alone. It will grow colder rather than hotter.' If we want to stay 'burning' in our Christian faith, it will be easier to do so alongside other burning coals, rather than trying to glow apart from the fire.

Secondly, public worship is a training centre. Church worship fails if it reinforces our sense that God is only 'in here', and not 'out there', if it merely sucks us into a whirlpool of church activities. Instead, it should be a centre equipping us for the business of living. No mountaineer would think of climbing Everest without essential equipment. Similarly, no Christian can sustain the arduous climb of living counter-culturally without being trained and equipped. Church should be about pushing us, better trained and equipped, into the week ahead. It should send us into our neighbourhoods and workplaces energized, refreshed, with a clearer sense of how we will encounter Christ in the world.

Third, public worship should be quality time the church spends with Christ. My wife would be rightly surprised if I took her out for a candlelit meal, spent the evening giving her my undivided love and attention, and then proceeded to ignore her the rest of the week. No – quality time spent with a loved one does not detract from the rest of life. It resources it and makes it more real. It reassures the loved one that in the uneventful and mundane times, the love and commitment is no less real. It reassures me that my partner is no less my partner when I am out at work or away from home. The love expressed during our quality time has a sustaining power to it.

Similarly, public worship is the time when the Church, the 'bride' of Christ (see Revelation 21) spends quality time with her 'bridegroom'. It is a moment of intense encounter which, far from denying the relationship which is there the rest of the time, dramatizes it in concentrated form.

In public worship, we do many things: we strengthen relationships with each other, learn new songs, new liturgies, new prayers, new insights about God. We rethink our personal values, try to gain new perspectives on our lives and work. But all these are secondary. Most of all, in public worship we encounter Christ. We spend quality time with him. Worship has no purpose or goal beyond encounter. Certainly it is not (as I heard one evangelical minister describe it) a warm-up act for the all-important sermon. Worship is the church's quality time with God. It is faith on the spiral of wonder.

We reflected earlier on the wonder felt by those who encountered Christ in Scripture. It was a mixture of astonishment, loving attraction and a shiver of awe bordering on fear. Authentic encounter with Christ in worship should evoke similar feelings in us.

In practice, our divided Church has tended to divide up spiritual wonder, parcelling it out between different traditions, each claiming we have a full experience of worship. The Pentecostal and Charismatic traditions

109

are strong on love and intimacy; Protestants on Scripture and personal holiness; Orthodoxy and Catholicism focus on awe before Christ's majesty. But all these emphases are needed.

Some of the most wonder-filled believers I meet are those who have begun to find the best insights of other traditions, while keeping what is best in their own. The Catholic who discovers the intimacy of Pentecostal worship. The Evangelical who finds in the sacraments a fresh sense of mystery and reverence. The Orthodox who falls in love with Christ for the first time. The Pentecostal who discovers the value of liturgy and the church year. The Baptist who discovers contemplative prayer. The Anglo-Catholic whose stern categories are blown away by a jovial gust of the Spirit.

This should not surprise us. Many of the most wonder-filled, inspirational Christians have combined a warmed evangelical heart and passionate evangelistic zeal with a 'high church' awe and reverence: Celtic saints such as Columba, Aidan and Cuthbert; Francis of Assisi, John and Charles Wesley, G. K. Chesterton, C. S. Lewis. The unravelled strand we each hold is real, but incomplete. The Church is at its strongest when it binds together all the strands of its 'woven cord'.[5]

But whatever tradition of worship we belong to, however many traditions we bind together, any worship which is not centred upon encounter remains a hollow shell. Without that sense of standing, wonder-struck, before Christ, Charismatic worship degenerates into emotional froth, Catholicism into dead ritual, Evangelicalism into a head-trip, Anglicanism into civic pride and social superiority, Orthodoxy into gaudy archaisms, and Calvinism into a finger-wagging fatalism. Without encounter, even the renewed, catholic evangelicalism many of us are working towards, could end up blending the worst aspects of all church traditions: a frothy, moralistic ritualism. With encounter each tradition, or mixture of traditions, is an invitation to wonder.

Worship leaders or ministers are doing more than leading a service. They are drawing us into the wonder-filled encounter of a relationship, without which there is no true worship, whatever the style.

Personal prayer

If public worship is quality time between Christ and his Church, personal prayer is quality time between Christ and each individual alone. It is making space for encounter. This might be in regular blocks of time, in brief prayers scattered through the day, in permanent gratitude.

Again, the issue is not technique or style. It is encounter. For many people, the focus of prayer is what it does for them: bringing them feelings of calm, a sense of perspective, an air of spirituality. But this is starting in the wrong place. Prayer is about the wonder of relationship. A single, hesitant word in the presence of a loved one carries more power and intimacy than the finest rhetoric spoken to a wall.

Jesus' parable comparing the fluent prayer of the religious leader with the stumbling apology of the tax collector (Luke 18.9–14) speaks of his attitude to our prayer. Being real is more important than being religious. In fact, in the New Testament, the main obstacle to real encounter is being professionally and slickly religious. Focus not on your own competence, but on the one you are encountering.

There is another, more subtle way in which personal prayer is about encounter. The distinctive Christian insight into God is that he is one, but in three distinct 'persons': Father, Son and Spirit. There is already communication and love within the Trinity. And we, as believers, have the very Spirit of Christ living in us.

111

The Spirit joins us to Christ (this is Paul's argument in Romans 8). So prayer is not simply something we do. It is allowing the Spirit of Christ to communicate through us to the Father, calling him '*Abba*', just as Jesus did (Romans 8.15). Prayer is an activity within the life of God himself, but – as people united with Christ – we have the privilege of being a channel through which this happens. This is mind-boggling to contemplate. But it underlines the same point. Prayer is not about technique. It is about encounter.

Bible study

As we read eye-witness accounts of Christ's life and teaching, death and resurrection, we stand in the place of those who first saw, heard and touched him. We cannot meet Jesus in the flesh. But we can soak our minds in the stories and letters of those who did. To read the New Testament is to be allowed to see with the wonder-filled eyes of those who first met him. It is to share their experience of encounter.

However, surveys reveal a consistently low level of regular Bible study, even among Christians.[6] If we are not concerned enough to look through the eyes of those who saw Christ, we should not be surprised that we fail to see him ourselves.

Here we find the importance of the preacher. Preaching achieves many things. It can be about passing on facts, telling stories, moving the emotions, challenging lifestyles, helping build a sense of identity and community. But these are secondary to its central purpose, which is to bring alive the Scriptures, to enable people to encounter Christ for themselves. The preacher at his best is an unobtrusive shoe-horn, easing us into the shoes of those who first met Jesus.

Sacraments

The two sacraments instituted by Christ, baptism and Holy Communion, are centred on encounter. A sacrament is a visible, physical sign of an invisible, spiritual reality. It is God taking ordinary things of the world – water, bread, wine – and using them as a means of encounter with himself.

At baptism, we celebrate a death. The waters of baptism dramatize both a washing away and the death by drowning of an old self. For Paul, baptism is sharing in the death and resurrection of Christ himself – he describes Christians as 'having been buried with him in baptism and raised with him through your faith in the power of God' (Colossians 2.12). Paul is quite clear: baptism is not just a declaration of our faith in God (though it can include this), or a merely symbolic act (although it is full of powerful symbolism). It is a real, sacramental moment, by which God actually does something in us: 'Or don't you know that all of us who were baptized into Christ Jesus were baptized into his death? We were therefore buried with him through baptism' (Romans 6.3–4).

So baptism involves the encounter of being united with Christ in his dying and rising again. It is also the sacrament through which we join the Church, Christ's 'body' (1 Corinthians 12.13). It is our moment of incorporation into the universal body of Christ. We begin to encounter Christ in each other.

Similarly, Paul writes of sharing in Holy Communion in terms of real encounter: 'Is not the cup of thanksgiving for which we give thanks a participation in the blood of Christ? And is not the bread that we break a participation in the body of Christ?' (1 Corinthians 10.16). The Communion service we join in week by week is full of reminders that what we are about

113

is encounter. These include the response, 'The Lord is here. His Spirit is with us.' And the 'Holy, holy, holy' reminds us of Isaiah's awe-struck encounter with God in his Temple (Isaiah 6). In Communion, those who never met Christ in the flesh are nevertheless united with him and his sacrifice. Communion mediates real encounter with Christ. This is not only a Catholic and Orthodox understanding. It is also the mainstream Evangelical position – that of Luther, Calvin and Wesley.

Holy Communion too carries a horizontal dimension of encounter: as we meet together around the Lord's Table and share one bread, we are united with his people, fellow-members of the body of Christ (1 Corinthians 10.17).

Sacraments bring about encounter, but never automatically or magically. A response of faith is needed. To kiss is to use our lips as a means of encounter. But the encounter is only real when the heart is engaged. Just so, the sacraments mediate encounter with Christ – but only in a context of living faith.

Worship and encounter: some conclusions

Some will want to add another category of encounter in worship: experiencing the power of the Spirit directly, perhaps during a 'time of ministry'. Many people find such occasions a time of moving encounter with God. But I believe it would be a mistake to place the Spirit's power in a category apart from the rest. The whole point of Christian lifestyle, public worship, personal prayer, Bible study and the sacraments is that *these* are places of encounter with Christ by his Spirit.

Some people believe the real business of encounter happens when the formal part of the service has ended, when the falling over, weeping and shaking begins. Their journey to church, talking to their neighbour, singing, teaching, praying and receiving of bread and wine are little more than a dull prelude. But this is a flat refusal to encounter Christ in most of the places he is to be found. It is brushing aside a five-course, *cordon-bleu* meal, because you have heard there may be a dish of mints at the end.

To find faith on the spiral of wonder is to encounter Christ, with awe, astonishment and love. And the place we find this is in an ordinary Christian life aflame with worship: in lifestyle, singing, prayer, study and sacrament.

GRATITUDE

The spiral of wonder turns not only through encounter, but also gratitude. In the life of faith, the places we find encounter fuel thankfulness. As we learn to discern the presence of Christ in our everyday lives, we discover glimpses of the primal experience of Eden: gratitude at the sheer wonder of life, the gift of each other, the gratuitous creativity of God. As we worship together in song, prayer and liturgy, and through the church year, we retell each moment in the story of redemption, and we give thanks.

In prayer our bottom line is gratitude: for who God is and what he has done. As we read the Scriptures and hear them expounded, we retell the story of God and his people as our own story. As we receive the sacraments of grace, we recall with thanks key points in that story, and enter into them ourselves: the Exodus and crossing of the Red Sea, the baptism of Jesus, the meal in the upper room, the death, resurrection and ascension of Jesus, the sending of the Holy Spirit. One of the historic names for the Holy Communion is 'Eucharist', which comes from a Greek word meaning 'grateful'.

COMMITMENT

Yet, as we look at the average church congregation, wonder is rarely the first thing to strike us. We see teenage boys fidgeting their way through the service; the woman who returns to her gossiping the moment the service has ended; the single mum whose choice in men shows little of godly discernment; the man more concerned to look for a wife than for God. We see people whose motives for being there are, to say the least, mixed. We sit between the spiritual exhibitionist, the misery and the malcontent. And we are supposed to encounter Christ *here*?

If only we were in that spiritually alive church on the other side of town. If only our musician could keep in time. If only our service was less formal, more formal, less simplistic, or more charismatic. If only . . .

But wait. See what is happening? No sooner have we listed the places of encounter with Christ, than we proceed to idealize and spiritualize them. In practice, we end up sidestepping the very encounters we seek. Christ tells us that we encounter him in 'the least of these' in society? Fine. The next time we come across a genuinely deserving ex-prisoner who needs a little help to get back on his feet, maybe we'll help him. But don't ask us to talk to the weirdo who sits next to us in church . . .

We encounter Christ in public worship? Fine, but just think how much better it would be if we could get a better organist/choir/saxophonist/disc-jockey (delete according to worship tradition). We encounter Christ in the sacraments? Fine, but we wish we had a dramatic conversion story, topped off by a moving full immersion baptism . . . And we do wish we used a different Communion wine . . .

Remember Mr Shoulderman, who looks over your

116

shoulder at parties, scanning the room for better talent? And remember the rampant 'If Onlys' in our imaginations? Both are as alive and well in our faith-life as in our attitudes to place and time: always telling us wonder is elsewhere. Telling us that real spirituality is anywhere other than where we are right now, with all our doubts, confusions, mixed motives, our second-rate church and uninspiring minister.

Try, just for a moment, to break this cycle. Try, just for a few seconds, to take God at his word. Think: my daily life is an arena where I meet Christ. I encounter him in the most embarrassing members of my congregation. As I pray he is there, listening for my every breath. As I read the Bible I gaze in awe-struck wonder at Christ, face to face. In my baptism, I am united with Christ in his death and resurrection. As I eat the bread and wine of Holy Communion, I participate in the very life of God himself. Let us commit ourselves to finding him in these places.

Spiritual wonder involves commitment. In part, this means a foundational commitment to Christ himself. Like any intimate relationship, this commitment must be passionate and single-minded. To settle for anything less is to settle for second-best. Such energetic devotion to Christ rarely creeps upon us unawares. As we noted in Chapter One, we rarely drift unawares into joy, commitment or wonder. But we can easily drift into indifference. It is as if we were standing on a downward escalator. To do nothing is to move slowly backwards. In this case, we drift into the unwonder of spiritual indifference. We progress by taking energetic jumps.

Commitment usually progresses by leaps – big steps of deepening trust. This includes the big jump of the 'outsider' with no previous awareness of Christ, and the smaller steps of an 'insider' raised in an atmosphere of faith.[7] For insiders, there may never have been a moment when they questioned that Christ was their Lord and Saviour. But even for them, steps of deepening commitment are still vital. They themselves do not stay the same. They are constantly changing and maturing. They need to keep rediscovering their faith in Christ afresh, reapplying it to each new phase of life: childhood, adolescence, young adulthood, and so on. Sometimes these rediscoveries and reapplications will feel like very big steps indeed. Even for the insider, to stand still is to descend into unwonder.

Spiritual wonder, then, means wholehearted commitment to Christ. But it also involves another type of commitment. And this, if anything, is harder than the first. We need to be committed to encountering Christ in all the places he says he is to be found. So much easier to be committed to a super-spiritual Neverland of holy livers, fervent worshippers and perfect preachers; to be committed to a pure, 'invisible' Church, which bestrides the ages, banners unfurled. But this is commitment to a mirage. The real work of spiritual commitment is messy and littered with compromise. It involves sitting next to people in strange clothes, who often sing out of tune. The body of Christ is unsettlingly real and everyday.

Encounter happens, but it doesn't necessarily happen where and when we choose. And it doesn't necessarily happen among the sort of people we feel comfortable with.

CHAPTER SIX

WHERE THE SPIRALS END

For there is good news yet to hear and fine things to
   be seen
Before we go to Paradise by way of Kensal Green.
(G. K. Chesterton, The Rolling English Road)

Life on a spiral

We have seen how living a life of wonder or unwonder
is like moving in a spiral. This is because a spiral
makes two types of movement simultaneously. One
is a circular motion. Life on the spiral of wonder turns
through encounter, gratitude and commitment – each
fuelling the next. And the spiral of unwonder turns
through indifference, fantasy and withdrawal. Again,
each place on the spiral fuels that which follows. But a
spiral is not a circle. It moves not only round and
round, but also onwards. Unlike a circle, it never covers
the same ground twice. Just like our lives, it is always
moving on, ever deeper into wonder or unwonder.

In our lives we make any number of choices which
move us along one spiral or the other. It usually doesn't
take long to spot which spiral a person has chosen. Even
allowing for the temporary ups and downs of mood and
circumstances, we can tell the difference between the
two. The one betrays herself by a twinkle in the eye
and a spring in the step; she sees life as an adventure of

discovery; she routinely counts her blessings; she is passionate about life and faith. The other is fundamentally jaded and cynical; he has seen it all; life holds no surprises for him; he has outgrown childlike faith.

We all know people like these. And we know that, barring conversions, the passing of time merely hardens attitudes. The most wonder-filled, caring people I have met are elderly. So are the most bitter and selfish. This is no more than we should expect: old age finds us a long way down the road we have been choosing to travel for all the years that have gone before. Wonder is a choice. And a lifetime's choices end up evident for all to see.

The place where the spirals end is death. There, all that we have been comes to nothing. We might have spent our lives on a spiral of wonder or unwonder but 'the rest', as Shakespeare's Hamlet says, 'is silence'.

Or is it? Try, for a moment, to imagine what a life might look like if the spirals of wonder and unwonder did not stop at death, as the atheist fondly imagines. What if they spiral on for ever? And what sort of people might we become if we carry on spiralling on into either wonder or unwonder, for all eternity?

What, in other words, if God keeps allowing us to choose which spiral we are on, even after death, and we become more and more creatures of wonder or unwonder . . . *ad infinitum*? Such questions, with their intriguing mix of theology and conjecture, are at the heart of one of the spiritual classics of the twentieth century: C. S. Lewis's *The Great Divorce*.

THE GREAT DIVORCE

Lewis's novel was written in 1945 and first published the following year, in an England just beginning to recover from the ravages of the Second World War. The 'divorce' of the title refers to the great gulf between heaven and hell which is the theme of the story.

Two points of background might help explain the context of Lewis's novel. The first comes from the English artist–poet William Blake, who wrote cryptically in a poem about the 'Marriage of Heaven and Hell'. No, says Lewis, heaven and hell are divorcees: eternally separated, never to be reconciled.

The second is from the fourteenth-century Italian poet Dante Alighieri whose masterpiece, *The Divine Comedy*, portrays the author's journey from hell to paradise. While Dante's guide through the afterlife is the Roman poet Virgil, Lewis's is the Victorian novelist George MacDonald, whose fantasy writings played a crucial role in Lewis's own conversion to Christianity. Much of the book's theology comes from the narrator's conversations with his wiser, older guide.

The plot of *The Great Divorce* is simple enough. In a dream, the narrator joins a bus full of people from hell as they are taken on a day trip to the outer fringes of heaven. There, each is given an opportunity to change their ways. Each may remain in heaven, if they choose. Lewis draws a stark contrast between the environments of heaven and hell. His hell bears an uncanny resemblance to an endless grey, rainy day in London, whereas his heaven is bright and solid. Even on the very edge of heaven, the residents of hell are as wispy ghosts, while the Bright People of heaven are solid and real. As the story unfolds, it becomes clear that for all its apparently vast expanse, hell is but a small crack in the grass of heaven. This theme – that hell is something tiny and insubstantial, whereas heaven is big, real and wonder-filled – forms the spiritual geography against which the book's journey takes place.

However, the real interest in the book is less plot than characterization. We watch with the narrator as each day-tripper is confronted in turn by the reality of his or her own pettiness and self-obsession. Each is given the chance to turn their back on this twisted, hellish self, and be saved. These portraits give Lewis an opportunity to unleash the most hard-hitting satire anywhere in his writing.

There is the working man from London, always insisting he is a 'decent chap', demanding 'his rights', and staunchly refusing a heavenly grace which is so free and abundant that it extends to murderers:

> 'I haven't got my rights. I always done my best and I never done nothing wrong. And what I don't see is why I should be put below a bloody murderer like you.'
>
> 'Who knows whether you will be? Only be happy and come with me.'
>
> 'What do you keep on arguing for? I'm only telling you the sort of chap I am. I only want my rights. I'm not asking for anyone's bleeding charity.'[1]

Then there is the tall, grey-haired ghost, who sees all the apparent joys of heaven as a cruel joke by some nameless authority to torment the likes of him. He is an arch-cynic, who has so convinced himself that every experience and place will be a disappointment that he refuses even to contemplate staying:

> I never saw one of these bright mornings that didn't turn to rain later on. And, by gum, when it does rain here! Ah, you hadn't thought of that? It hadn't occurred to you that with the sort of water they have here every raindrop will make a hole in you, like a machine-gun bullet. That's their little joke, you see. First of all tantalise you with ground you can't walk on and water you can't drink and then drill you full of holes. But they won't catch *me* that way.[2]

Funniest and most biting of all Lewis's satires is the pompous, liberal bishop who has ended up in hell. Even confronted with the solid joys of heaven, he still would rather cling to the woolly open-mindedness that characterized his ministry on earth: 'Ah, but we must all interpret those beautiful words in our own way! For me there is no such thing as a final answer. The free wind of inquiry must *always* continue to blow through the mind, must it not?'[3]

Lewis gives the satirical dagger a final twist by showing how some religious-minded people would rather discuss faith in the abstract than encounter God himself – even into eternity:

> Bless my soul, I'd nearly forgotten. Of course I can't come with you. I have to be back next Friday to read a paper. We have a little Theological Society down there. Oh yes! there is plenty of intellectual life. Not of a very high quality, perhaps. One notices a certain lack of grip – a certain confusion of mind. That is where I can be of some use to them.[4]

The moral of *The Great Divorce* is stated by Lewis's guide, George MacDonald: heaven and hell are not states that begin after death. Each is simply a natural extension of choices made during an earthly life: 'All that are in Hell, choose it. Without that self-choice there could be no Hell. No soul that seriously and constantly desires joy will ever miss it. Those who seek find. To those who knock it is opened.'[5]

Contesting the divorce

Lewis's imaginative and humorous fable is clearly relevant to our discussion of the spirals of wonder and unwonder. Wonder spirals on into eternity. So does unwonder. And the places where each ends up are what

123

Christians have traditionally described as heaven and hell.

But *The Great Divorce* is, after all, only a fable. The book itself claims to be nothing more than a dream. Are we really at liberty to see it as a realistic portrait of eternity? First, we must admit that aspects of the book owe more to Lewis's personal preference than a dispassionate reflection on the afterlife. As in most of Lewis's writing, the author reveals a clear preference for rural over urban life. His hell is a grey city, heaven a pastoral idyll (devotees of C. S. Lewis might like to compare the grim cities of Tashbaan in *The Horse and His Boy*, or London and Charn in *The Magician's Nephew*, with his rural idylls of Narnia and Archenland, or Venus in *Voyage to Venus*).

This bias clearly owes more to Lewis's own likes and dislikes than to the biblical portraits. In the Bible, by contrast, eternity with God is glimpsed as taking place in a vast, busy city: the New Jerusalem. It is a place full of energy, wealth, colour, style and celebration, into which all the kings of the earth will bring the finest artefacts of their cultures (Isaiah 60, Revelation 21).

Likewise, Lewis simplifies the scriptural understanding of heaven, glossing over a number of distinct aspects which characterize the biblical hope. In the Bible, heaven is not only God's 'personal space', where he rules in majesty (Matthew 6.9). It is also presented as a kind of waiting room, where believers who die may rest and wait (Revelation 6.9–11), until the coming of a magnificent 'new heaven and a new earth' (Revelation 21.1), at the end of the present age. This new era is inaugurated by the return of Christ to the earth in glory (Philippians 3.20), the resurrection of the body (similar to the resurrected body of Jesus himself: 1 Corinthians 15.12–58, Philippians 3.20–21), and a final judgement. At that point, the present separation of heaven and earth will be done away with, and believers will live as embodied people on a renewed earth (Revelation 21.1–4). Truly, the meek will then inherit the earth, just as Jesus promised (Matthew 5.5). The ultimate hope of believers is to live in a New Jerusalem, a place of excitement from which every tear has been wiped away (Revelation 21.3–8). Clearly, Lewis could not fit the entire biblical imagery or chronology into a short piece of fiction.

Lewis's picture is also incomplete in its presentation of human freedom of choice. In *The Great Divorce* we find a great deal about the processes of human choosing, but little about the things (or, rather, the One) being chosen.

My 'freedom' to buy a new shirt in reality depends on many factors beyond myself, including the worker who made the shirt, the retailer who sold it, and the employer who pays my salary. Likewise, Lewis dwells more on our destiny solely as a matter of our choosing, less on the fact that we are only free to choose life and wonder because God has gloriously made these options available to us. And he says little about the content of these options (the place of the cross and resurrection, God's grace, and so on).

No doubt this incompleteness is due to the medium in which Lewis is writing. He is, after all, writing a fantasy novel and not theology. He writes, as any novelist must, 'from below', exploring the drama of human freedom and motivations, rather than 'from above', about the scope and origins of the options on offer. This is entirely valid, as long as we recognize that his picture is partial. We must not end up concluding, like some philosophers in recent decades, that it is our act of choosing alone that determines our identity and destiny. Still, Lewis is right. The choices we make, from the options on offer, are crucial in shaping our future.

So we need to grant C. S. Lewis a large measure of poetic licence in his evocation of heaven and his handling of complex issues of free will. He says as much in his preface:

I beg readers to remember that this is a fantasy. It has of course – or I intended it to have – a moral. But the transmortal conditions are solely an imaginative supposal: they are not even a guess or a speculation at what may actually await us.[6]

But how plausible is his hell? Clearly, Lewis's grey, wet streets are simply local colour, to add a backdrop of misery to the scene. The most distinctive insight of Lewis's portrait of hell is found in the words of George MacDonald:

Hell is a state of mind – ye never said a truer word. And every state of mind, left to itself, every shutting up of the creature within the dungeon of its own mind – is, in the end, Hell. But Heaven is not a state of mind. Heaven is reality itself.[7]

In other words, for Lewis hell is an eternal descent into the emptiness of a self cut off from joy and wonder. It is an eternal, godless narcissism.

Lewis may have come across the germ of this idea in the writing of G. K. Chesterton who, along with George MacDonald, was a major Christian influence on the young Lewis. An early story involving Chesterton's detective–priest, Father Brown, is entitled 'The Sign of the Broken Sword'. In it, Father Brown discusses Dante's *Inferno*, and reflects on the nature of crime. His definition sounds familiar:

Anyhow, there is this about such evil, that it opens door after door in hell, and always into smaller and smaller chambers. This is the real case against crime, that a man does not become wilder and wilder, but only meaner and meaner.[8]

Christian theology has traditionally recognized two different understandings of hell, each claiming biblical support. One sees hell as a place of eternal anguish. In 1998 a French used-car salesman, Marc Rheims, was so convinced he was going to go to hell when he died that he insisted on being buried in a fireproof suit. And medieval artists had a field-day painting the flames and red, pitchforked demons who would be one's neighbours in this type of hell. Such literalism, however, is not vital to this understanding. The flames might simply be a potent metaphor to convey the painful reality of an eternal, conscious separation from God.

The other conventional image of hell is annihilation. Its proponents, including such prominent evangelicals as John Stott and John Wenham, claim the most natural reading of the biblical imagery is that hell means the extinction of life, in contrast to eternal life with God. Just as objects thrown in the fire do not remain there unconsumed but are burned up, so the biblical fires of hell are a metaphor for final death.[9]

Lewis offers a third option: hell as freely chosen isolation, an eternity on the spiral of unwonder.

Hell and unwonder
Lewis offers an alternative picture of hell, which seems both biblically admissible and psychologically plausible. It is admissible in biblical terms because it does justice to certain key scriptural notions: the idea of hell as separation from God; that human free-will is real and not illusory; the biblical insight that God is a God of love, who desires that none should perish; the

insistence of Jesus and Paul that the experiences of salvation and lostness begin now.

But most unnerving about Lewis's hell is its psychological plausibility, once we have begun to grasp the dynamic of the spiral of unwonder. The person living on this spiral has learned cynical indifference to everything: the place they are in, the present moment, God, people, work, things. They vaguely dream that things are probably better somewhere else, but refuse to take the steps of commitment necessary to find that wonder. They withdraw from encounter with everything that might draw them beyond themselves: God, other people, the world around them.

The person on the spiral of unwonder, Chesterton's criminal, Lewis's person in hell, are all fundamentally in the same place: passing through an ever-receding series of doorways into smaller and smaller rooms, deeper and deeper into themselves, further and further away from encounter.

Heaven and wonder

Lewis's heaven, admittedly sketchy, partial and coloured by the author's personal taste, also seems biblically admissible and psychologically plausible. In biblical terms, it does justice to the major scriptural ideas: an eternity in the presence of God; that all the wrongs and injustices of earth will be righted; that all who choose salvation will find it; that the New Jerusalem will be a solid place of light, joy and celebration.

Like Lewis's portrait of hell, the picture of heaven in *The Great Divorce* also carries psychological plausibility. It is a convincing picture of the spiral of wonder, tumbling on into a joyful eternity.

One of the most moving moments of the novel is when the narrator sees a grand procession in honour of a great woman of dazzling brightness and unutterable beauty. We are led to expect that it might be none other than Mary, mother of Jesus. But when the narrator questions his guide about the woman's identity he receives an unexpected response: '"Not at all," said he. "It's someone ye'll never have heard of. Her name was Sarah Smith and she lived at Golders Green".'[10]

It turns out that the earthly life of this unknown woman, in a residential London suburb known at the time only for its ordinariness and poor Eastern European immigrants, had been one of selfless devotion to others. She loved and cared for children in her neighbourhood, but not in a way that made them resent their own parents; she affirmed local men, but not in such a way as to draw them away from their own wives; she cared for the animals that crossed her path too – local pets and wild animals alike.

Here, then, is the insight at the heart of *The Great Divorce*. The book is not intended to be an A to Z of the afterlife. It is a dream-like tale with a simple moral: eternity begins not at some unspecified future date: it begins now. The central and defining statement of the book is spoken by George MacDonald – that hell is an eternal descent into the self, but heaven is an openness to divine wonder which draws us beyond ourselves: 'There are only two kinds of people in the end: those who say to God, "Thy will be done," and those to whom God says, in the end, "Thy will be done." All that are in Hell, choose it.'[11]

CHOOSING A SPIRAL

In his central emphasis on our choices determining our destiny, Lewis not only echoes the clear teachings of Jesus and Paul. He also affirms everything we have said about the spirals of wonder and unwonder.

Wonder is a gift of God. But it is also a choice we

make each day of our lives. It means making a deliber-
ate choice of intimate encounter rather than casual
indifference; heartfelt gratitude rather than escapist
fantasy; and passionate commitment rather than
cynical indifference. It means an awe-struck and loving
encounter with here, with now, and – ultimately – with
the One who is himself at the very heart of wonder.

Try embracing the gift of wonder for a day. Then a
week. Experience for yourself what a difference it
makes. Then imagine your life ten years from today:
after ten years lived on the spiral of unwonder, and on
the spiral of wonder. Then picture 20 years, and 30, on
each spiral. Then imagine what sort of person you will
be by the end of your life, the product of a lifetime's
accumulated choosing of wonder or unwonder. Finally,
allow your imagination to extend those spirals into
eternity.

The person living on the spiral of wonder is the
person who has learned to read the story of their lives
backwards. They have caught a glimpse of the sort of
person they might end up becoming, if they carry on
along a particular path. They know that every step they
choose to take moves them deeper into wonder or
unwonder.

Choosing life

A potent image from the Old Testament comes to mind.
Moses is close to death. He and the people of Israel
have been wandering in the wilderness for 40 years,
and finally they are on the verge of entering the
promised land of Canaan. As he speaks to the people,
Moses sets before them a stark choice of two paths:
'This day I call heaven and earth as witnesses against
you, that I have set before you life and death, blessings
and curses. Now choose life, so that you and your
children may live' (Deuteronomy 30.19).

This same fundamental choice is offered to each of us. Choose to embrace God's gift of life: a life of faith and passion which spirals through days, weeks and years of wonder. A life which continues to spiral on into a wild, joyful eternity.

FOUR EXERCISES TO
HELP RESTORE
LOST WONDER

SENSE DAYS

Take a day to focus on just one of your body's senses: sight, hearing, touch, smell or taste. Pay particular attention to everything which that sense encounters, things you normally take for granted. A Touch Day might notice the softness of the bedsheets, the heat of the shower, the texture of the tablecloth, the feel of the fabric in your clothing, the roughness of the wall in front of your home, the texture of the bark on nearby trees.

A Smell Day might focus on the aroma of your morning coffee, your shampoo, smells in the air outside: fragrances of flowers and grass, food aromas from restaurants and people's homes. And less pleasant smells: exhaust fumes, drains, rubbish bins in the street. Each Sense Day, use your chosen sense with a fresh sharpness. Thank God both for your own capacity to sense, and all the things your senses encounter in the world. Alternatively, have a Sense Day imagining how you would manage that day if you were to lose one of your senses – such as sight or hearing. Again, allow this to generate thankfulness.

PILGRIM IN MY OWN PARISH

Take a day to encounter afresh the place where you live. Walk around the streets, looking more intently than you have ever looked before: at buildings, plants, people, and so on. See what new things you can find. Go to a local library or museum, speak to a long-time resident, consult a book, to learn about the history of the area. Learn to celebrate and be grateful for the distinctiveness of the area you live in.

LIVING IN THE PRESENCE OF CHRIST

In the morning, before the busyness of the day begins, sit quietly. If necessary, take some time breathing deeply to calm your body down. Think over one of the biblical promises of the constant presence of the Spirit of Christ: 'And surely I am with you always, to the very end of the age' (Matthew 28.20); 'Unless I go away, the Counsellor will not come to you; but if I go, I will send him to you' (John 16.7); 'Do you not know that your body is a temple of the Holy Spirit, who is in you, whom you have received from God?' (1 Corinthians 6.19). Thank God that his Spirit really is in you, right now.

Reflect on what the presence of the Spirit might mean in the coming day. Think about what you expect to do today, and reflect on what it means that Christ is there with you. This is the heart of Christian spirituality: a normal life open to the presence and promptings of the Spirit.

FINDING CHRIST IN OTHERS

The writer to the Hebrews suggests some of us have actually met spiritual beings unawares: 'Do not forget to entertain strangers, for by doing so some people have entertained angels without knowing it' (Hebrews 13.2). Jesus tells us that as we serve the needy we are actually serving him (Matthew 25.31–46).

As you meet others today (at home, work, church, or wherever), be open to finding something of God in each encounter. Warning: it probably won't feel like a 'spiritual' encounter at all! At the end of the day, reflect on your meetings with people during the past day. Were you challenged by something somebody said? Did they give you something: an object, a new insight, a feeling, affection? Did they offer you a chance to live out the life of service Christ calls you to? Did you meet an 'angel' today? Even Christ himself? How might you change the ways you relate in future, if you want to follow more closely the pattern of Christ's own encounters with people?

NOTES

1. THE SPIRAL OF UNWONDER

1. Details from report, 'Millionaire too bored to live', *The Daily Telegraph*, 4 June 1998.
2. Cited in I. G. Barber, *Religion and Science* (SCM 1998), p. 59.
3. *Macbeth*, Act 5, scene 5, line 16.
4. G. Keillor, *We Are Still Married* (Faber and Faber 1989).
5. *Love and Death* (1975 film).
6. Annual worldwide expenditure on advertising has been predicted to reach $1 trillion by the year 2000. See E. Clark, *The Want Makers* (Hodder & Stoughton 1988), p. 12.
7. N. Farndale, 'Dinner with a friend', *The Sunday Telegraph Magazine*, 21 June 1998, p. 11.
8. C. Hibbert, *The English: A Social History 1066–1945* (Grafton 1987), pp. 386, 580.

2. THE SPIRAL OF WONDER

1. G. K. Chesterton, *Autobiography* (1936). In *Collected Works of G. K. Chesterton* (Ignatius Press 1988), vol. XVI, p. 97.
2. C. Kingsley, *Daily Thoughts* (Macmillan 1884), p. 155.
3. W. Temple, *Nature, Man and God* (Macmillan 1934), p. 156.
4. A. Einstein, *Ideas and Opinions* (Souvenir Press 1973), p. 11.
5. Cited in M. Mayne, *This Sunrise of Wonder* (Harper Collins Fount 1995), p. 109.
6. G. A. Studdert-Kennedy, *The New Man in Christ* (Hodder & Stoughton 1932), p. 132.

135

7. C. Carretto, *The God Who Comes* (Darton, Longman & Todd 1974), p. 5.
8. R. May, *Man's Search For Himself* (George Allen & Unwin 1953), p. 212.
9. T. Browne, *Religio Medici* (1642), p. 1.
10. D. H. Lawrence, *Phoenix II* (Heinemann 1968), p. 598.
11. E. Underhill, *The Wisdom of Evelyn Underhill* (Mowbray 1951), p. 11.
12. Cited in S. Patin, *Monet: The Ultimate Impressionist* (Thames & Hudson 1991), p. 109.
13. M. Starkey, *God, Sex and Generation X: A Search for Lost Wonder* (SPCK/Triangle 1997), p. 1.
14. M. Mayne, *This Sunrise of Wonder* (Harper Collins Fount 1995), p. 15.
15. Cited in R. P. Martin, *Philippians* (Marshall, Morgan & Scott 1976), p. 162.

3. THE WONDER OF HERE

1. M. Riddell, *Threshold of the Future* (SPCK 1998), p. 103.
2. As described by Robert Lancham, a court official of Queen Elizabeth. See C. Hibbert, *The English: A Social History 1066–1945* (Grafton 1987), p. 199.
3. A. Dillard, *Pilgrim at Tinker Creek*. In *The Annie Dillard Reader* (Harper Collins 1994), p. 294.
4. A. Dillard, *Pilgrim at Tinker Creek*. In *The Annie Dillard Reader* (Harper Collins 1994), p. 284.
5. A. Dillard, *Pilgrim at Tinker Creek*. In *The Annie Dillard Reader* (Harper Collins 1994), p. 288.
6. N. Holmes, *Looking for God* (Triangle 1998).
7. N. Holmes, *Looking for God* (Triangle 1998), p. 24.
8. N. Holmes, *Looking for God* (Triangle 1998), p. 91.
9. See E. Peterson, *Leap Over a Wall: Earthly Spirituality for Everyday Christians* (HarperSanFrancisco 1997), particularly chapters 7–9.
10. E. de Waal, *Celtic Light* (Harper Collins Fount, 1997), p. 55.
11. E. de Waal, *Celtic Light* (Harper Collins Fount, 1997), p. 73.
12. O. Davies and F. Bowie (eds), *Celtic Christian Spirituality: an Anthology of Medieval and Modern Sources* (SPCK 1995), p. 29.
13. E. de Waal, *Celtic Light* (Harper Collins Fount, 1997), p. 78.

14. E. de Waal (ed.), *The Celtic Vision: Selections from the Carmina Gadelica* (Darton, Longman & Todd 1988).
15. D. Spriggs, *God at the End of the Century: Encounters in Today's Culture* (The Bible Society 1996).
16. D. Spriggs, *God at the End of the Century: Encounters in Today's Culture* (The Bible Society 1996), p. 80.
17. D. Spriggs, *God at the End of the Century: Encounters in Today's Culture* (The Bible Society 1996), p. 81.
18. G. K. Chesterton, *Orthodoxy* (1988). In *Collected Works of G. K. Chesterton* (Ignatius Press 1986), vol. 1, p. 270.

4. THE WONDER OF NOW

1. C. Plantinga, 'Can God be Trusted?', *Christianity Today*, 15 June 1998, p. 45.
2. W. H. Auden, 'For the Time Being', in *Collected Longer Poems* (Faber and Faber 1968), p. 158.
3. W. H. Auden, 'For the Time Being', in *Collected Longer Poems* (Faber and Faber 1968), p. 158.
4. R. L. Stevenson, *Travels With a Donkey* (1879).
5. A. C. Swinburne, *Hymn to Proserpine* (1866).
6. R. Burridge, *Four Gospels, One Jesus?* (SPCK 1994), p. 36.
7. C. S. Lewis, *Mere Christianity* (Fontana 1955), pp. 116–17.

5. AT THE HEART OF WONDER

1. M. Riddell, *Threshold of the Future* (SPCK 1998), p. 3.
2. R. E. Davies, *I Will Pour Out My Spirit: A History and Theology of Revivals and Evangelical Awakenings* (Monarch 1992), p. 202.
3. E. Peterson, *Leap Over a Wall: Earthy Spirituality for Everyday Christians* (HarperSanFrancisco), p. 9.
4. See P. Yancey, *Disappointment With God* (Harper Collins), particularly Part One.
5. See M. Mitton, *Restoring the Woven Cord* (DLT 1995).
6. A Bible Society survey of the UK from 1995 shows that 15 per cent of regular churchgoers have never opened a Bible, and 17 per cent have not opened one in the last year. Fifteen per cent read it daily, and 19 per cent read it once a week or more.
A poll in the USA (Princeton Religious Center, 100

Questions and Answers: Religion in America 1989)
found that in a country where around 40 per cent of the
population attend church, 11 per cent of people read the
Bible every day. In 1990, the Barna Research Group found
that among those claiming to be 'born-again Christians',
18 per cent read the Bible every day, but 23 per cent
admitted they never opened a Bible.

7. These categories are from David Wells. See D. Wells,
*Turning to God: Biblical Conversion in the Modern
World* (Paternoster Press 1989).

6. Where the Spirals End

1. C. S. Lewis, *The Great Divorce* (1946) (paperback edition:
Fontana Books 1972), p. 32.
2. C. S. Lewis, *The Great Divorce* (1946) (paperback edition:
Fontana Books 1972), pp. 52–3.
3. C. S. Lewis, *The Great Divorce* (1946) (paperback edition:
Fontana Books 1972), p. 40.
4. C. S. Lewis, *The Great Divorce* (1946) (paperback edition:
Fontana Books 1972), p. 42.
5. C. S. Lewis, *The Great Divorce* (1946) (paperback edition:
Fontana Books 1972), p. 67.
6. C. S. Lewis, *The Great Divorce* (1946) (paperback edition:
Fontana Books 1972), p. 9.
7. C. S. Lewis, *The Great Divorce* (1946) (paperback edition:
Fontana Books 1972), p. 63.
8. G. K. Chesterton, 'The Sign of the Broken Sword', in *The
Innocence of Father Brown* (1911). Collected in *The Father
Brown Stories* (Folio 1996), pp. 180–81.
9. See D. L. Edwards and J. Stott, *Essentials* (Hodder &
Stoughton 1988), pp. 313–20. J. Wenham, *The Enigma of
Evil* (Eagle 1994), Chapter 6. And, more fully, W. Fudge,
The Fire That Consumes (Paternoster 1994).
10. C. S. Lewis, *The Great Divorce* (1946) (paperback edition:
Fontana Books 1972), p. 98.
11. C. S. Lewis, *The Great Divorce* (1946) (paperback edition:
Fontana Books 1972), pp. 66–7.